Knockma Inkwells

A Second Collection of Poems,
Short Stories, Articles and Wise Sayings

2013   Kieran and Padraic Reaney

Knockma Inkwells
Copyright © 2022 by Kieran and Padraic Reaney

All rights reserved. No part of this book may be reproduced or
transmitted in any form or by any means, electronic or mechanical,
including photocopying, recording, or by any information storage and
retrieval system without express written permission from the author,
except in the case of brief quotations embodied in critical reviews
and certain other noncommercial uses permitted by copyright law.

Printed in the United States of America.

Brilliant Books Literary
137 Forest Park Lane Thomasville
North Carolina 27360 USA

This book is dedicated to Knockma Hill,
and all the people, who love, enjoy
and support the Arts.

Introduction

Knockma Inkwells is a follow up to our first book Feelings Within which was highly acclaimed locally, nationality and internationally. Knockma Inkwells has poems, short stories, articles, wise sayings and many colour photographs. Several issues are dealt with, and told as they are, and analysed, going back years and decades, and in some cases blending fact with creativity. The huges social change, all across the board, that has taken place in Ireland, beginning in 1960 and culminating in the birth and eventually the death of the Celtic Tiger era, is bravely and courageously explored, and also a study into the deep psyché of the Irish people. Since the start of this new decade, the country is in transition, and probably could be called the Lonely Cub era.

Knockma Inkwells also highlights and gives information on some great Irish writers' down through the years. A special mention to David Burke, Editor of The Tuam Herald, for always supporting the Arts. I told him one time that I had an idea for writing an article, and his sound advice was, "If you fel like writing, then certainty go ahead." A special word of thanks also to Jim Carney, Sport and Farming Editor of The Tuam Herald, and indeed to all the local press and media.

Kieran and Padraic are former members of Tuam Athletic Club and Donaghpatrick/Kilcoona Athletic Club. They are also members of Ballinfoyle Pioneer Group, and wish to thank everyone that kept inquiring about this book for months back. Padraic planned the layout of the book and Kieran took several of the photographs. Go Raibh Maith Agat to one and all.

Kieran and Padraic Reaney

E-mail: reaney04@nokiamail.com

Table of Contents

Emily Lawless (1845-1913):
Masterclass Writer Near Knockma 11
Passitiviy And Passion 19
Bygone Days 21
Embers Entwined 23
A Fresh Slice Of Life 24
Precious Time 24
Bubbling Beauty Bursts 25
Jailbreak 27
Don't Get Caught 27
Generous, Genuine Girl 28
In Your Dreams 29
First Time 29
Claustrophobia 30
Corporal Punishment, Education And Fear 31
Don't Act On It 33
Contentment 34
Farmer Debs 35
No Bone China 36
Do You Inherit Land Or Does Land Inherit You? 37
Welcome To The Human Race 38
Evolving Backwards 39
Heatwave 40
Modernised Farming Or Cold Egotism 41
Stayin' Alive, Slane Alive 42
Radiation And Its Consequences 44
No Pope, No Hope 47
Doctor's Orders 48
Lovers 50
No Pullet 50
Victims 51
The Nature Of Things 51
Saddle Sore 53
The Middle Man Deserted 53
Ye're All Stone Mad 54
Epitaph 55
Almost Perfect 55
Mass Rocks, Hedge Schools And Milestones 56

Late Sixties	57
How're Ya Doin' Sham?	58
Tuam Remembered	58
Having Your Cake Or Eating It	59
The Person That Laughs Last Laughs Most	59
Played Puck	60
Lost Maiden	61
From Learner Driver To Full Throttle	61
Galway's Dream	63
July Sunday	65
Liberalism Blazing	65
Destiny	66
Avoiding Atheism	67
Reading Between The Wrinkles	68
Getting Old	70
By God We Suffered	71
Lascivious Lassie	72
Ye'll Vote For Them Again?	73
Live For The Moment	74
Happiness	77
Sadness	77
Anger	78
Fear	78
SARAH Is Good For You	79
Reality Bites	79
Eyes Of The Soul	80
Able, Available And Willing	82
Connacht Calling	83
Bleeding Spirits	83
Learning Life's Lessons	85
Cream Always Comes To The Top	86
Memories Of Alfred The Great	87
No Strings Attached	88
It's The Way It Has Gone	89
Costly Mistakes Are Breeding Cynicism	90
Gospel Truth	91
Greatest Let Down Of All	92
Pitiful Politics	93
Sizzling Similarities	94
City Bird	95
Stains Of Sin	96
Galway…Races	97

Horses For Courses	97
Losing It In Galway City	99
Table Quiz	100
Out Of It	101
Reincarnation	102
Porter-Head-Work	103
Only Messin'	104
Pole Dance	104
Hard-Up Oul' Lads	106
Girl Power	107
Making Cents Of It All	108
All The Same	109
Dream Girl	110
History, But What About Her Story?	110
Pork Chopped	112
The Bar Maid	113
Change Isn't Always A Good Thing	114
Young Heart Skipping A Beat	115
The Choice Is Yours	115
Deep Soul	117
Hail Glorious St. Patrick	118
Back To Learning	121
Life's A Bitch And Then He Married Wan	121
Broke and Broken	122
Soulful Scenarios	123
Throw't In Ref!	124
Come On! Caman!	125
We'll Win It	126

Emily Lawless (1845-1913): Masterclass Writer Near Knockma

History, just after it has happened, is the hardest time to analyse it. The so-called Celtic Tiger years of the late 20th century and eary years of this 21st century, will always be remembered as the time when Ireland reached its zenith in growth and prosperity, after it was gradually built up, for over 150 years since the Famine. Unfortunately this boom period flattered to deceive, and eventually led to a collapsed economy, total chaos, and ultimately to bankruptcy for the "Dear Little Isle" on the Western Ocean.

Around a hundred years prior to this, in the late 1800s and early part of the 1900s occurred probably the most exciting and fruitful time ever for writing in this country, namely the Revival of Irish Writing. Astonishingly a lot of these gifted writers and their work had connections to the Galway and Mayo area, Castlehackett in Catherlistrane, Coole Park in Gort and Cong in County Mayo. One of these writers' was Emily Lawless form Castlehackett House, the virtuoso woman of Irish Writing, which it seems had been failed to be recognised and remmebered by Irish history.

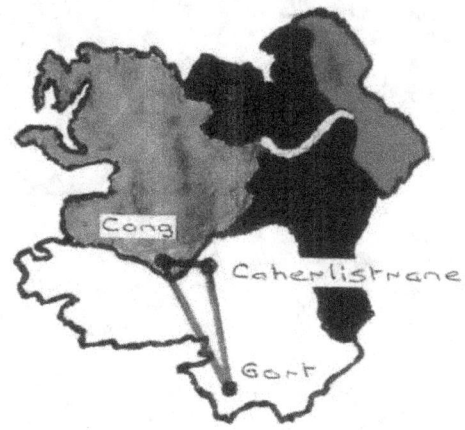

Testimonial Triangle. *Catherlistrane in North Co. Galway, Gort in South Co. Galway and Cong in South Co. Mayo, connected by top class, excellent Literature – as part of the astounding Art – Heritage. History and Culture. The other three Connacht counties, Roscommon (coloured in blue). Sligo (brown) and Leitrim (red) are also very much linked to these brilliant, outstanding attributes, that make the West of Ireland a very unique and special place. With the Irish psyché or soul if you like, running so unbelievably deep, the well of inspiration will always be filled to the brain, and the West will remain truly awake. Artwork by Padraic Reaney.*

Emily Lawless was born on the 17th June 1845, at Lyons House, Ardclough, Co. Kildare, the third of nine children. Her parents were Elizabeth Kirwan of Castlehackett House and Edward Lawless, Lord Cloncurry, a wealthy Anglo-Irish nobleman. Emily as a child and even in later years spent several summers at her mother's home in Castlehackett.

A relative of Emily, General Lawless, was with Wolfe Tone when they interviewed Napoleon. Her father was a friend of Daniel O'Connell. And the first President of Ireland, Douglas Hyde, wrote frequently about the Kirwan's. He visited Caherlistrane in the early 1900s, and was presented with items of musical heritage by Pat Costello of Feeragh.

Ms.Lawless loved literature and she spent a lot of time in her father's library. She was the only member of the Kirwan's to pursue a career in writing.She was slim and petite and had com-coloured hair, and loved the outdoors and horses, and used to ride with the hunt. A friend of her mother, the novelist Margaret Oliphant encouraged Emily to write fiction.

Castlehackett House *as it is today, but it was in the old Castlehackett House, before it was destroyed by fire in 1923, that Emily Lawless spent the summers with her mother Elizabeth Kirwan, for several of her earlier years.*

Ms.Lawless wrote 16 books of fictions, biography, history, nature studies and 3 collections of poetry, 19 books in total, which were widely read at the time. The Belfast Central Public Library and Belfast Linenhall hold many of her books today. In the New York newspaper, the United Irishman, on 30th April 1892, it ws stated that Ms. Lawless was 'A Great Irish Novelist' commenting on her 7th book Grania which was published in 1892. Jeremiah O'Donovan Rossa was the editor of the newspaper.

Grania was set on the Aran Islands but J.M Synge on reading the book wasn't too happy as he believed that Ms. Lawless may never have spent any time on the islands, perhaps because she was one of the gentry, but she actually lived some time there.

Ms. Lawless was introduced to Lady Augusta Gregory – co-founder of the Abbey Theatre. Dublin – at St. Cleran's in Craughwell, which was the home of Irish film director John Huston and his daughter, actress Angelica Huston, from 1954 to 1971. Lady Gregory and William Butler Yeats had a long and productive association for 37 years, and they were great friends of Ms. Lawless, who visited them many times in Coole Park in Gort. She would even stay with them for a weekend occassionally. W.B Yeats and Lady Gregory used to write about Knokcma and the Kirwan's.

On two different occassions Lady Gregory described Emily as 'gentle' and 'genius'. W.B. Yeats had Ms. Lawless in his top list of writers' from this era, but Yeats and Ms. Lawless didn't always see eye to eye. There was tension between them for the obvious reason they were in competition as regards writing.

But there were tough times in Ms. Lawless' life. Her father and two of her sisters commited suicide. Lady Gregory was well aware that these tragedies would stand Ms. Lawless in good stead in writing terms as nearly all creative writing comes from pain. Perhaps the more a writer has suffered the better their writing will be. A sculptural portrait of Ms. Lawless' father, Edward, was for some years prominently displayed in the National Gallery of Ireland.

Lady Gregory was seven years younger than Ms.Lawless, born near Kilchreest, not far from Gort in 1852. She was married to Sir William and they had one child, Robert. W.B. Yeats bought the Norman Tower House, Thoor Ballylee – within walking distance of Coole Park – for £35 and lived there with his wife Georgie Hyde-Lees and their two children. Coole Park was a haven for writers as we all know from the famous Autograph Tree: Lady Gregory, Douglas Hyde, AE(George Russell),Augustus John, Sean O'Casey, George Bernard Shaw,J.M. Synge and W.B. Yeatst.

Thoor Ballylee, *the Norman Tower House, within walking distance of Coole Park in Gort, where W. B. Yeats wrote some of his greatest poetry.*

Hackett's Castle, *in front of Knockma Hill, another Norman Tower House, was built by the Hackett's who were Norman in the late 14th century, is similar to Thoor Ballylee.*

Sir William Wilde began building a holiday home, which he called Moytura Lodge, on the shores of Lough Corrib, near Cong in Co. Mayo, in 1864. Sir William, his wife, Lady Wilde and their two sons, Oscar and Willie, used to spend the summers there. They also had a third child, a daughter, Isola. Sir William, before his marriage to Lady Wilde, had three other children, a son and two daughters. The two daughters in heartbreaking adversity lost their lives, after getting badly burned when a fire started at a party.

Sir William Wilde, Lady Wilde and W.B. Yeats visited Knockma, and Lady Wilde was one of several writers that wrote about the magical hill. Sir William once said that Lough Hackett in Caherlistrane, was a great place for coarse fishing, and described the crannóg (a man-made island) in the lake, as the best example of one in the whole Lough Corrib area. He also said that the scenic beauty of Cong, Lough Corrib, Connemara and that area, stretched all the way over to Headford and Knockma Hill. Sir William wrote the book Lough Corrib, Its Shores And Islands which was fist published in 1867.

Magic Door: *In 1859, behind this door, Emily Lawless walked through the field in front of Castlehackett House. This door is across the road from the car park at the foot of Knockma Hill. A few years later, Oscar Wilde and his brother Willie, played in the garden of their holiday home, Moytura Lodge in Cong, Co. Mayo, while staying with their parents, Sir William Wilde and Lady Wilde, who was also known as Speranza the poetess.*

Oscar Wilde, as well as being a great writer, at one stage did a painting of a view looking out over Lough Corrib from Moytura Lodge. Oscar and his brother Willie, as little boys, spent their time fishing on Lough Corrib, exploring the lake by boat with their father, Sir William, and playing in the garden. Oscar's first girlfriend was Florence Balcombe, and it lasted two years, but she left him, and married another writer, Bram Stoker, author of Dracula.

Sir William Wilde was a doctor as well as writer, antiquarian and statistician, and he dealt with an outbreak of cholera in Kilmaine. His grandparents' lived in Ballymagibbon, Cross, which is not far from Cong. On a visit to Cong, which is a while back, my brother Padraic and I were told that The Edge from U2 – probably the best rock band ever to come out of Ireland – and his wife, were living in Moytura Lodge when we visited.

Church of St. John The Baptist of The White Church, *as it is also known, on the outskirts of Headford, but actually in the parish of Caherlistrane. Oscar Wilde's ancestors, the Flynn's of Ballymagibbon, Cross, near Cong are buried here.*

Ms. Lawless at one stage had the same publishers as James Joyce. He was married to Galway city woman Nora Barnacle, and he visited Galway in 1912, going to Rahoon and the Galway Races. His wife, Nora, had a profound influence on his work.

Ms. Lawless' best work is the novel Hurrish set in the land-war torn landscape of the Burren, in Co. Clare, is a story of love and betrayal, involving the murder of a landlord. William Gladstone said that this book instructed him on the land question in Ireland. Ms. Lawless dedicated this book to Margaret Oliphant.

Ms. Lawless' ability to describe various topics is fantastic. Below is an extract from Hurrish – which was first published in 1886 – describing the Burren, which is part of the first paragraph, and sets the trend for the rest of the book.

"You picture them dotted over with flocks of sheep, which nibble the short sweet grass, and frisk in their idle youth over with the little declivities. If here and there a rib or so of rock protrudes, they merely seem to be foils to the general smoothness. But these Burren hills are literally not clothed at all. They are startlingly, I may say scandalously, naked. From their base up to the battered turret of rock which serves as a summit, not a patch, not a streak, not an indication even, of green is often to be found in the whole extent. On others athin sprinkling of grass struggles upward for a few hundred feet, and in valleys and hollows, where the washings of the rocks have accumulated, a grass grows, famous all over cattle-feeding Ireland for its powers of fattening. So, too, in the long vertical rifts or fissures which everywhere cross and recross its surface, maiden-hair ferns and small tender-petalled flowers unfurl, out of reach of the cruel blasts. These do not, however, affect the general impression, which is that of nakedness personified – not comparative, but absolute."

Emily Lawless' best work the novel Hurrish *which was first published in 1886.*

From the extract above it is easy to know that Ms. Lawless was a poetess as well as novelist, an the description above, could also as easily be interpreted as an extended metaphor in poetic parlance. Ms. Lawless, even though she was from a Protestant ascendancy background, and combined nationalist feelings with unionist sympathies, she had great talent as a writer, and conributed significantly to the Revival of Irish Writing, but she never got the praise or credit she so richly deserved. At the present day amazingly and ironically, and the omnipresence of Information Technology, not much has changed in a hundred years or more.

Emily Lawless towards the end of her life was in declining health, becoming more depressed and addicted to morphine. In my opinion she was Ireland's greatest ever female writer. She passed away on the 19th October 1913, aged 68 years, which is a hundred years ago this year. Emily's 19 books are listed below.

> A Chelsea Householder (1882)
> A Millionaire's Cousin (1885)
> Ireland (1885)
> Hurrish (1886)
> Major Lawrence FLS (1887)
> Plain Frances Mowbray And Other Tales (1889)
> With Essex In Ireland (1890)
> Grania (1892)
> Maelcho (1894)

A Colonel Of The Empire (1895)
Traits And Confidences (1898)
Atlantic Rhymes & Rhythms (1898)
A Garden Diary (1901)
With The Wild Geese (1902)
Maria Edgeworth (1904)
Book Of Gilly (1906)
The Point Of View (1909)
The Race Of Castlebar (1914) – co-authored with Shan Bullock
The Inalienable Heritage (1914)

Kieran Reaney

Maura Darcy, Kieran Reaney, Nuala Murray and Helen Gavin, pictured after receiving their Access to Third Level Certificates from the Regional Higher Education Network at N.U.I.G.

If a person in life finds something is very hard to do, there are only two ways they will do it, if they have to or they want it badly enough. – **Kieran Reaney.**

Passitiviy And Passion

Paddy the Irishman and his wife Patricia the Irishwoman attempting to do eroticism is like a sumo wrestler trying to do synchronised swimming. Paddy thinks the only way to make 'the earth move' is to hire a JCB! If Paddy began making love with Patricia, and an Italian man began making love with his wife, both starting at the same time, when the Italian couple would just be getting 'into it right', Patricia would be fast asleep and Paddy would be snoring.

The following morning, for the purpose of keeping Paddy's fragile ego 'massaged', Patricia would tell him that, "It's the competing that counts." Paddy and Patricia had more hang-ups about 'the wild thing' than a telephone system has as regards unwanted calls. One night Paddy was out for a few drinks in a local pub and he got talking to another man called Patrick, who was a single gent.

"What do you think about marriage?" Patrick asks Paddy. "I suppose it's all right," replies Paddy, and he continues, "But there's one thing about it, the hours are very long." "Right you are," says Patrick, and then he asks, "Why is a Psychiatrist always wary of changing a light-bulb?" "You've caught me there," says Paddy. Then Patrick says, with a sly grin on his face, "He's never sure does the light-bulb want to change." "Jays I want to change," says Paddy, "That's for feckin' sure."

Then Patrick said, "A beautiful girl in the city told me this joke around a week ago." He continued, "Why is a married man very fed up?" "Beats me," said Paddy, but Patrick knew that he was jumping inside with excitement and anticipation, to hear what was a beautiful girl's take on it. Then Patrick said, "A married man is living in a country that sucks, he's living a life that sucks, he's working in a job that sucks, and he's married to a prude that won't suck!" They both laugh uncontrollably and then Paddy says, "How did I get 'sucked' into it?" Patrick then says, "Love is blind, but the neighbours aren't!" They both continue laughing heartily.

It goes without saying that later that night Paddy srolled home from 'the watering hole' more confused and unhappy than ever. He was thinking about the following day, which would more than likely be a bitterly cold, dark and dull day – maybe even pouring rain – in the depths of winter, when Patricia and himself would be on the sideline, cheering on their local Junior C hurling team, in a bottom of the league match.

In these harsh situations enthusiasm doesn't come easy, and a bit of hash wouldn't go astra, in a desperate bid to lift the spirits, and indeed the sliotar. However, where there's a life there's hope, and where there's hope there's life. Against all the odds Paddy and Patricia stuggle on, releasing years of anger and frustration, with loud passionate shouts, "Pull on it, puck it, give them timber."

After decades of 'hard' labour, maybe lack of 'hard' labour, Paddy can't take any more, he is at his wits' end, and he has no option but to see a 'Shrink'. This Master of the Mind tells Paddy to lie up on the couch, and try to talk about his problems and concerns. At that point, almost miraculously, Paddy gets a morsel of funny inspiration and says with a confident smile, "Sure that's the whole problem, me wife won't let me up on the coach!"

Padraic Reaney

A cute single lad knows how to get all the benefits of marriage, without marriage, and avoid all the losses. This is what modern Irish society has done. – **Padraic Reaney.**

Telephatic Theologians

Padraic and Kieran Reaney, aged 10, after their Confirmation in Caherlistrane Church in 1973.

What advantage has a lad playing the game of his life over a lad playing in the forwards for a football team? A lad playing the game of life can change the goalposts whenever he wants to, and that's how he plays the game of his life. – **Kieran Reaney.**

Bygone Days

Oh! God take me back.
To the oats and haystack.
The haggard and the hay-shed.
The fields and the homestead.

The plough upturns the soil.
The hungry sea gulls in toil.
The mower cuts the hay.
Where the quiet corncrake lay.

Blowing th bugle that shrills.
The red jacket that thrills.
The fox crosses the road.
Evicted from his humble abode.

Semi circles swing the scythe.
The ladybird flies the fright.
The thresher and the chaff
The camaraderie and the craic.

The boreen and the blackberries.
Climbing walls and picking cherries.
Brideogs and wren boys keen.
The hazelnuts and Hallowe'en.

The sugar beet and crown.
Depths of winter don't frown.
Ice so slow to thaw.
Potatoes under clay and straw.

The flood and white foam.
Now ne'er can we roam.
The closing curtains of night.
The spinning wheel and insight.

Kieran Reaney

Older and Wiser: *Advantages and disadvantages of getting older include an older person being able to live one day at a time because their energy levels have gone down somewhat. When they go to bed they don't worry because they're too tired. They don't waken up an hour earlier in the morning before the alarm clock goes off, full of enthusiasm for another day, because they can live for the moment.*

If a girl isn't for them they can take it with a pinch of salt, even though they know this is bad for their heart they say to themselves: "Sure no-one could eat chips without a bit of a flavour in them!" — **Kieran Reaney.**

St. Thérèse of Lisieux
"I will spend my Heaven doing good on earth."

Inspirational Thoughts: In the course of her final illness, Thérèse said to her sisters: "I feel that my mission is about to begin, my mission to make a God loved as I love Him; to teach others my little way . . . it is the way of spiritual childhood . . . the surrender of the little child who sleeps without fear in its Father's arms." Every pope of the 20th century has recommened the Faithful to take the words of St. Thérèse to heart, to read her autobiography. Here are few relevant quotations from the various popes: "She rediscovered the central message of the Gospel." Her's is "The secret of sanctity." "We would study her in order to copy her." Thérèse takes to heart and puts into practice the insisten words of Jesus: Unless you change and become like little children, you shall not enter the Kingdom of God."

Embers Entwined

Sigh for her.
Vie for her.
Lie for her.
Cry for her.

Hear for her.
Fear for her.
Near for her.
Dear for her.

Kind for her.
Bind for her.
Wind for her.
Mind for her.

Kieran Reaney

A lad will only pursue a girl fully when he cannot do without her. – **Kieran Reaney.**

Trilogy: In the following 3 poems the soul of the female of the species from the little girl, aged 5, the girl in her mid teens and the girl, aged 20 is explored.

A Fresh Slice Of Life

Early Summer, lunch break, sitting in car.
Relaxing, eating salad sandwiches, soft drink.
Observing, looking, noticing, little girl enters picture.
White bicycle helmet, pink jumper, blue denim jeans.

Pink and white cool runners, slowly, shakily, surely.
Pushing hard, getting power, from within, from God.
Tender pedals of life turning, planet Earth revolving .
Day, night, brightness, darkness, her dad beside her.

Supporting her, Guardian Angel, protecting her.
Unaware, innocent of big, bad, mad evil world.
Genuinely, sincerly, hoping that she is lucky enough,
To avoid oceans of pain, hurt heartache, that is,

Part and parcel, of human life, for most people.
Wheels of a young, vulnerable, beautiful life.
Little lady, twisting into motion.
Our Lady, be good to her, watch over her.

Padraic Reaney

Precious Time

Saturday night, first dance, sweet sixteen.
Parents gone to Mass, grand-mother holds the fort .
Her guardian angel, ravishing beautiful girl.
All day getting ready to go out, excited, anxious.

Nerves tingling slightly, charm bracelet chiming.,
She throws back her charcoal mane of black hair.
A huge fire burning within, a wild tiger's smooth skin.
A magical soft rug, an endless labyrinth of opportunity.

The world, her oyster, begging to be explored, tasted.
Innocent daisy chains, necklaces, locked in childhood.
Frozen by mechanical hands, another era, life's cycle.
Peddling to change, full of eager anticipation.

Putting the final touches to her make-up.
Up for the challenge, chasing elusive, butter-fly dream.
She walks confidently into the kitchen.
Does a twirl, her head spinning.

And stands tall in her sharp stilettoes.
Her slim body shivering with enthusiasm and desire.
Wearing silk stockings, a discreet white blouse.
A sensuous black mini-skirt and passionate red jacket.

Dressed to thrill, she blusrts out,
"What do you think, Gran?"
Her Granny says, "You're absolutely gorgeous,
You'll be 'the belle of the ball',
You seductress from Venus."
"Thanks, Gran, you're a dote, I love you."

Kissing her warmly on the cheek, she then says,
"Is it that time, I have to run or I'll be late."
She looks quickly at the grand-father clock on the wall.
Which is at this point in time, her only enemy.

Padraic Reaney

Bubbling Beauty Bursts

Life, like bubble on ocean, can burst at any moment.
However, "Youth must have its fling."
Young girl, vivacious, voluptuous, precocious.
Exploding with passion.
Wild with wickedness, ironically harmless.

Pulsating, a time-bomb, brimful with energy.
Enlightened enthusiasm.
Un-controllable, raw, un-cultured sexuality, high spirited.
Outrageous, shocking sensuality, high spirited.

A child at heart, a naive angel, no prayers said,
Easy prey, jungle out there, vicious animals,

Dark life, obscured, hidden, crouched in long grass,
Waiting anxiously to pounce, dimmed by alcohol,
No resistance, seduced quickly, grand fellow.

Hot, steamy, a lubricated piston, a mind of its own.
"It was made for dancing baby," mechanincal manoeuvres.
Engineered by nature, penetrates the sweet nectar.
"Steady up, slow down, this isn't Formula One.

You'll blow the engine in it, take yout time man."
Flesh-pot, erupting into orgasmic spasms of ecstasy.
The non-stop action, the rhythm and timing,
In total harmony, in unison, inside the
Magical chamber, of a combustion engine.

Ticking over beuatifully, reved up to a
Crescendo of euphoria, it all geos terribly wrong,
Loss of innocence, too much spilt milk.
"Familiarity breeding contempt", it all turns sour.
Eventually she's chewed up, her soul spat out.

Severely burned in circle of destruction.
Chance of citeog ring gone forever.
Idyllic life-style in the castle of adventure is over.
Her red cloak is ripped off, her tears flow.

The solid ice-cube of her whole being melting to
Water, gas choking, she's cruelly thrown outside
Heaven's Gate, and into the moat.
The wolves from Hell are watching her, like hungry
Hawks, they can't wait to satisfy their 'fear gorta'.

Padraic Reaney

A promiscuous girl is only wanted for a bit of fun, but no-one wants to bring her to the altar. - **Kieran Reaney**

Jailbreak

The train splits the snow mounds deep.
The plough furrows the stubborn stubble, weep.
Barbed wire tears the knee and jaw.
Full metal jacket, makers of the law.

The tracker dogs, no control of paw.
Tear through the rubble, claw by claw.
The split stubble, under shallow water, still.
A hollow pipe, the silent breathes fill.

The hallucinations and chaos, did not abide.
Spirit and freezing water, did not subside.
Jumps a carriage, a leg in pain.
Now does rest, where the hobo's lain.

Kieran Reaney

A successful person is like a gunslinger, when you least expect it, or when yout back is turned or at any time, a little boy or anyone else can say, "Draw, Mister!" - **Kieran Reaney.**

Don't Get Caught

Fishy business, a man will lie for it, cry for it.
Pay for it, crash a car for it.
Get beaten up by a jealous husband for it.
Live together for it, get engaged for it.

Fake romance for it, get married for it.
Seduce for it, listen to emotional confusion for it.
Pretend to love for it, fight for it, die for it.
Give land for it, loose money for it.

Lose his soul for it, get a girl into trouble for it.
Get STD's for it, get conned for it.
Wine and dine for it, cheat for it.
Get into crime for it.

A roll in the hay, he'll take his chance.
Was it worth it? "Every form of refuge has its price."

Padraic Reaney

In this country as standards, or lack of them, continue to get lower, knickers come down faster. **– Kieran Reaney**

Generous, Genuine Girl

Two little girls, aged around five, are playing a simple, innocent board game. Towards the end, one of them is confused and does not know which move to make. The other girl, in a compassionate tone of voice, says, "Move that one quickly and you'll beat me." The other girl does this immediately, and her friend says, "You've won." Then she pats her on the back and they both start cheering joyfully.

Padraic Reaney

A person that is bad minded, bitter and begrudging, and trying to keep other people back, are only keeping themselves back. **– Kieran Reaney.**

The Mossfort Namestone.

In Your Dreams

We danced that night on Fernsod Hill.
The moon fate, brought light and quill.
She spun around, I held her still.
Her staring eyes, besotted by the thrill.

The cockerel breaks dawn, the dissecting shrill.
The corn awaits, at my father's mill.
The water buckets, she goes to fill.
And bids good morning, "Ah! I'm in!"

Kieran Reaney

A very talented person is like a tree with a thousand branches. People in power and authority will cut off some of the branches but will be unable to cut them all. The buds will multiply and new branches will spring forth. **– Kieran Reaney.**

First Time

"We'll hop into the back seat now," said Mary Ellen. Then, Pateen O'Daye began to think to himself: "We most certainly will not. What is this New Age we're livin' in? Our backward country, it's not the roaring' twenties or swingin' sixties. I'm not that type of a man at all. Why did I drive into this laneway in the Morris Minor? What am I doin' at all? She'll have her brazier off before I know it and she'll try to pull the trousers off me. Pete McCafferkey would kill me for goin' on with his youngest daughter. Tomorrow when I'm walking through the fields, I'll be praying for a crop failure. On this autumn evening I haven't even the oats cut, and only one trailer of turf. I'm only here for a kiss and a cuddle. Ah! Or as macho lads in the local town would say, "A piss in a puddle." Tonight Pateen O'Daye is goin' all the way. Why wouldn't he, isn't he entitled to his 'bitten fun'. All men will take it when they get it on a plate, and Pateen is goin' to be no different. It's quite cat that won't drink milk. After this, if word leaks out, you won't be a stud or super-hero, but you'll simply have joined the Club. Oh! Mary Ellen, what did I do? Well, God forgive me. There will be a young Pateen O'Daye ramblin' round the fields inside a year, and I not having enough money to pay all the bills."

Kieran Reaney

A couple going out together that aren't married, if the girl gets into trouble, if, and when, her boyfriend marries her, is when he gets into trouble, classic pay-back time. **– Kieran Reaney**

Claustrophobia

Down under, down pit, Paddy-land, the pits.
You left yout cushy, easy job in Green Ireland man,
Down here you have to put 'the pick' to the brogeen,
Three shovels in front of you, take your pick.

No more pratees, no lumps of gold, lumps of labour.
Kango hammer, hammer action ,kangaroo
Hopping , nerves jumping.
A tough oul' station, perspiring profusely, dehydrated.

Little light, losing energy, stuck in hell-hole.
Outrageous fear, buried alive,birds,Shelaghs, be mine.
The mind, a mine-field, tip-toeing cautiously .
Ready to blow you up, to put you arse over head.

Slow it down to an old time waltz, slow hand lover.
Dancing on egg-shells, careful movements, soul boiling.
You could fry them on rocks here, for Easter.

Vultures devouring them without salt, oestrogen rising.

Like cearc a fraoach, disppearing into the sky.
Crocodiles snapping viciously as they fade into
Oblivion, Faraway mountains are green but bare.
Hills going up, pills going down

Don't let dynamite explode in your hand.
Elusive dream turns into harsh nightmare,hold it
Together, Paddy, you'll never stick this, let him out.
Attractive bird flies out of cuckoo clock, alarm rings.
Radio comes on,Lazarus jump out of bed, "G'day!"

Padraic Reaney

The human mind can be a very dark piece of machinery. – **Padraic Reaney.**

Built and natural heritage in Mossfort.

Anyone that creates or performs art is a passionate person.— **Padraic Reaney**.

Corporal Punishment, Education And Fear

Irish schools, decades ago, torn by pain.
Teachers coercefully, forcefully,
Pushes pupil's head down angrily,
Into barrel of cold,freezing water,

Other pupil's head, violently, repeatedly,
Banged ferociously off pebble-dash wall.
Stone thrown aggressively at other pupil.
Hits him on the mouth, tooth out flying out.

Some pupil's thought that they had read the
Teacher like a book, that he was a soft touch,
During class one day,he makes a rare, stupid
And silly, untypical mistakes.

Macho, immature lad laughs his head off,
This goes straight to the teacher's head,
And he punches him viciously, putting him flying
Off his seat, "Teachers always right" in those days.

"Some day, out on the farm fields," teachers says,
"Ye see a dodgy lamb, looking weary, weak,
Pull the boot on him, kick the life out of him,
Bring him into class, boys,

We'll cut him up, see what he looks like,
On the inside, all the money farmers have,
Ye'll never miss him." You're wired to the
Moon man, primitive,bad,mad,evil,sick
Shameful Ireland.

Padraic Reaney

Some doors in the long corridors of the mind should never be opened. – **Padraic Reaney.**

Almost Heaven, North Galway, Knockma Mountain, Clare River.
This road, which starts at Teresa and Mary-Ann Creaven's house, was resurfaced in recent years, and links Ballintleva in Corofin with Glenshawk Hill in Caherlistrane. About half-way on this road there is a stile at a right-angled corner which is a back entrance to Castlehackett House.

Twice a child and once a man:*At the beginning of his life he is a child, then he grows up to be a mature, adult man and towards the end of his life , due to old age, he goes back to being a child.* – **Padraic Reaney.**

Don't Act On It

Seventy year old farmer, living alone
Helper nephew to get 'the place
"Islands In The stream",
Argument over trivial matter,
Escalates into a serious row,
Farmer says, "I' ll change the will."

Nephew goes 'cracked' with anger,
Overflowing, boiling, loses his head,
Trigger-happy, gets shotgun,
Take someone 'out' first,
Ask questions later,
'Riffles' farmer to another world.

From one lover of land to another,
Ha! Ha! Guards rush to the scene,
Come between, nephew taken away,
How did it all go wrong?
Quick Court case, nephew found
Guilty of mans-laughter.

Sentenced to years of imprisonment,
Dry up your tears.
That same 'Judge', quite possibly,
When he might become,
Outrageously angry, in his own
Personal life, may shoot several
People, in his own mind.

Or maybe even worse, but he would
Never even dream of doing it in
Reality, he never acts in haste,
That's why he's still the 'Judge',
And the nephew will have plenty
Of time 'behind bars',
To repent, at leisure.

Padraic Reaney

A friend or friends' only exist nominally. – **Kieran Reaney.**

Contentment

A taste of paradise and hell.
Contrasting, they have stood me well.
The blood flowed clear and bright.
The sweat dripped out of sight.

The audacity low, knee no cheer.
God's light was there to steer.
Languages are universal in the bed.
Glass of spirits, memories are she.

Kieran Reaney

In life bad days count just as much as good days, they are all added up. – **Padraic Reaney.**

Mechanical Horsepower replaces Live Horsepower. *The iconic Ferguson 20 Tractor from the mid-20th century gave the old workhorse a final rest and paved the way for all types of huge, heavy tractors, and all designs of complicated, sophisticated farm machinery in the years and decades thereafter.*

Farmer Debs

Macho like rhino.
Grey Ferguson 20 T.V.O
Danes, Deans and Deano.
Soccer creelers and peno.
Cigarettes, Bunny and Credo.
Lambs, shams and Donno.

Twenty pounds and gypo.
What? I don't know.
The garden to mow.
Paddy Doe, no hoe.
Boats will they row?
A trailer, no tow.

Clay pipes and meano.
Tie, no dicky bow.
John or Jane Doe.
She needs no dildo.
The better will flow.
On top, down below.

Where is lovely Zoe?
Drinking like a wino.
Walking away, no blow.
No friend or foe.
Hot, praying for snow.
"Keep it cool. Johno!"

Kieran Reaney

No Bone China

Li Wong was from China and married to Kim. They had two children, a little boy aged seven and a little girl aged eight. Li's mother also lived with them, and he worked very hard, but he hadn't that much money saved. He was unhappy, and one day a male friend suggested that they should move to Ireland because it was the time of the so-called Celtic Tiger.

Eventually the whole family moved to the place where, "The grass grows a greenest". They were only a few weeks in Ireland when Li's mother became incontinent. He brought her to the hospital and he told her he would go in first to see were they busy. Inside the door he met a student nurse and he said, "My mother is incontinent." "Very good." Replied the nurse, "Which country in Europe is she gone on her holidays?"

He sat down then to wait for a doctor, and a man beside him said, "What do you think of euthanasia?" "I suppose they're the same as the youth any place else," said Li. Then the doctor came and he would be left with a big bill. Li then decided that he would mind his mother at home.

That evening he went into a shop and told an attractive girl working there he would make love with her twice in a row. She laughed it off and said, "Two Wongs don't make a right!" Around that time their son and daughter were having a difficult time at school. The Irish kids seemed to be obssesed with one joke which they would tell several times every day, "What would you call a China man with one ball? Wan Hung Lo!"

Li was finding it hard enough to get a permanent job and he was beginning to get frustrated. One day he went to the bank to see had he much interest to get, but he was told it was only five cents. "What do you mean?" said Li. The bank teller said, "Fluctuations." "Fuck you Irish too," said Li.

Kieran Reaney

All aspects of life all over the world are very rarely what they seem. – ***Padraic Reaney.***

Do You Inherit Land Or Does Land Inherit You?

Down through the years, decades, centuries.
The Irish people were preoccupied with land.
Rural country people, farmers.
Tenants, and to a lesser extent,
Urban dwellers, living in towns and cities.

Part of the Gaelic tradition, way of life, psyché.
This mentality was probably due to the fact,
That for so long, they were denied ownership,
Of it by landlords, and so on.
Eventually when they got their own "hands" on it,

By God how they loved, adored and cherished it.
It was valuable, precious property, like gold dust.
And they were not going to let it go,
Without some fight.
This obsession with land is very deep,

As it is great security.
Land is passed on from generation to generation.
But it is deadly dangerous, and
Human life has been lost at times,
When people battle tooth and nail.

And go through hell or high water,
To get "Four Green Fields".
The law of the country, these people,
Believe in "The Law of the Land".
Especially after the "road frontage",

Buzz word came into it, in the boom times.
The wise person knows that,
At the end of the day,
You can't bring it with you, to the next life.
All you are going to have, in the final analysis is,

Six feet by three feet, prepared by,
"The poor crooked scythe, and spade",
In your small, graveyard resting plot.

Padraic Reaney

There are only two evil things in this world, men and women. – **Kieran Reaney.**

Welcome To The Human Race

Tea for two, two for tea.
Red or white wine, black or white.
Two sides of a coin, heads or tails.
Different takes on it, it takes two.
Two sides to every story.
"Too many cookes spoil the broth."

"Many hands make light work."
Pros and cons, it takes two to tango.
Your guess is as good as mine.
Black man walking on side of street.
Beautiful, tall, slim, blonde, fair-skinned girl,
By his side, dole queue of unemployed people,

Across the road, on the other side of the street.
Young lad gets frustrated, loses discipline, shouts out,
"Look at the cut of that opportunistic flute,
That hoor of a nigger boy is taking our lovely girl,
And whatever else he can get soft in Paddy-Land."

He replies angily, running like a scalded cat,
"Why don't these lazy hang around Paddies,
Get out there, move their hole and get a jog,
The sleepy buckoes have the country robbed."
They'd have this guts for garters, if they caught him.

Padraic Reaney

Unfortunately in this life, all over the world issues such as Racism, Discrimination, Bullying, Corruption, cash in brown envelopes, and the proverbial 'pull' – always a huge part of Irish life, not what you know but who you know – will be there for however long the human race exists. – **Kieran Reaney.**

Evolving Backwards

Jumpy farmer, nervous, insecure, not relaxed.
Inspired by meithal, "What's that?"
Due to cut-backs, law and order neglected.
Wild animals hammering, law of the jungle.

"Who's trying to sleep with my beautiful wife?"
"Hold on, where's my knuckle duster?"
"Who's that in the back-kitchen,
Trying to seduce my lovely daughter,

His trousers downl around his ankles?"
"Hold on, where are my boxing gloves?"
"He'll wake up with a crowd around him,
With a ball and chain locked to his ankle."

"Who's trying to evict me from my humble abode?"
"Hold on, where's my sharp slash-hook?"
"Who's trying to take my gander's paddock?"
"Hold on, where's my loaded musket?"

"Who's trying to steal my fat bullockeen?"
"Hold on, where's the bread-knife?"
"Who's trying to rob me of my few bob?"
"Hold on, where did I bury the hatchet?"

Aggression, violence, teach them a lesson.
Women holding on for a hero, "Who's that?"
The modern Ireland, not nice, not good, not pretty.
In a very bad place, a sick, evil hell-hoe.

Very little to hold on to, to cling to like a leech.
No leadership, no good example, people being destroyed.
Back to Neanderthal man, crying what have ye done?
"Hold on tight to your dreams", caveman.

Padraic Reaney

When a man is in bad form, he goes into his cave. When a man is in good form, he goes into a woman's cave. – ***Padraic Reaney.***

Heatwave

From Heavens it came,
Pony tail and mane.
The heat and humidity,
For days testing longevity.
Tar sizzling, bursting seams,
Scantily clad, day dreams.
Cool drinks, barbecue steams,
Shovels and ice creams.
All night until dawn,
A siesta late morn.

Sea gulls can rain,
Now only the pain.
Travelling, tired and unbowed,
Thunter and lighting aloud.
Lunch-boxes and school bags,
Replace 'hens' and 'stags'.
The rickshaw paved way,
On Cruise-boat, no booser,
Days we were looser.

Kieran Reaney

Cooked Up: *Apartment Blocks were part and parcel of the Celtic Tiger era. They were, and indeed continue to be social prisons, behind locked gates.* – **Padraic Reaney.**

Modernised Farming Or Cold Egotism

Sleeping on a harrow, Poet gone into dreamland.
Mid-twentieth century, Ferguson 20 Tractor.
New horse-power, replaces tired and weary,
Work-horse, once strong as a bull, now sad and lonely.

Pick-axe, spade, shovel, sickle, slash-hook, flail.
They never fail,take your pick. Picking of a crow-bar,
Sledge-hammer, tough manual work, hard graft.
Times changed, craft-work, kango hammer hopping.

Like a kangaroo, "What will this do to your nerves,
Jack?" Power tools, back-breaking labour,
Gradually taken out of it. Replaced by all types,
Of complicated machinery. Ironically the closure,

Of the four sugar factories, slated or tiled houses replaced,
Thatched cottages. Slatted sheds replace cow-sheds.
"Take full advantage of the grants available to you now,
Sir."Olden times, small families houses, big families, modern age,
Big houses, small families.Bogs, turf and peat,

Replaced by expensive oil heating. In later times,
The Rural Enterprise Protection Scheme, leave it as it is.
At one stage farmers were advised to reclaim land.
The whole thing went kilometres too far.

Monstrous tractors, sophisticated farm machinery.
Hi-luxes, 4x4s, Jeeps, quad bikes, ride-on
Lawn-mowers, not needed at all, all an excuse
In spending euros, or keeping down taxes,

Or impressing the proverbial Joneses.
The remarkable irony is, they're always preaching,
The 'beal bocht', the mind boggles.
In most cases the Banks probably paid for it.
Like lots of other things in this country.

Padraic Reaney

Breaking Wind: Two options that could be considered by farmers in the future wre Forestry Farming, if they want to branch out, or Wind Farming, if they *want to reduce anxiety. It is all about pillow talk, putting a few euros in the new Bank in this country, which is called Under the Pillow. Then he can sleep sound, provided he has a shotgun under the bed, or sleep like a cowboy, with his head on the money-filled, saddle-bag and one eye opened. Irish life has definitely become an eye-opener, everyone are winking in agreement. – **Padraic Reaney.***

Stayin' Alive, Slane Alive

Pete Burns, peat burns, not the best solid fuel in the world for heat though. Nora was sun-bathing and Heather, her younger sister, lying beside her, both girls day-dreaming. Turf accountants, tough accountants, violin players, music fiddlers, figure fiddlers, figure skating, vertical dancing, horizontal dancing, any gents to take us out at the weekend?

Dad Pete says. "Wake up, lassies, don't fall asleep anyway, or a bog lizard might get into your mouths." Nora jumps up suddenly and says as she rubs her tired eyes with her timid hands, "The bucks around here that are like lizards, they'd have their slimy tongues a yard down your throat before you'd know it, you'd be gasping for breath, they'd nearly choke you, the ignorant schmucks."

I leather hd now also come alive, and her older sister Nora says, as she hands her a bottle of cold tea, just after uncorking the paper stopper, that was stuffed down the neck of it, "Have a drop of tae, Heat." She replies abruptly, "The same out' story, you'd be as well off drinking bog-water. I'll go on the beer at the weekend, champagne or some craic like that."

Pete can feel the tension and frustration of his two daughters, and cutely slips into his calm, relaxed way, using coaxing techniques. "Have a few cuts of koskeen and hairy bacon sandwiches." Then Nora quips as she takes a sup of the magic bottle, "The men around here love a bit of hair on it all right!" They all begin to get in good form, and Nora continues, "I never came across a farmer that wasn't into a good cop of grass!" They all laughed heartily.

Then Heather said, as she took the sandwiches in hand, "Feic this country butter, you have to stay hours pounding the dash churn, trying to change milk into butter, and the end result isn't that hectic." She continued, "Jesus changed the water into wine in a split second, sure this oul' farming is all hard labour and nothing after it, you're glutons for punishment, there's no money in it."

Then she said, with a naughty look in her eyes, "Dad, why don't ye buy some of those bread spreads you'd see in the supermarkets, they're chape enough, and there's one thing about them, like a lot of birds in this locality, they spread very easily." Then Pete said, "They're as wild and out of control as the cearc a fraoach!" Tears of laughter were running down their legs.

She then continued, "What was that pea-brain at last Saturday night, after the dance ended, singing, "When I first said I loved only you Nora, and you said you loved only me." Nora replied quickly, "They'd say nothing to get inside your bloomers, sis." Pete then said as he was smiling, "Sure it's in the nature of the baeste!" Then Nora said, "I don't know about other girls, but I'm choosey about who I drop them for."

Heather then said in a soft, sheepish tone of voice, "But what about the handsome Frenchman, now living on the outskirts of the parish?" Nora quipped as she was getting excited, :That's a stallion of a different colour, he's welcome to take a look under my skirt any yime he feels like it." She then continued, "Ah! He's a man and a half, the sexy, confident and concentrated look in his eyes would burn a hole in yout drawers." Then Heather said, "The local ass-holes around here wouldn't hold a candle for him." They wouldn't keep the ball kicked out to him, sis," said Nora.

Pete was now on cue, and in the mood for a bit of kicking ass himself. "Bogman's Ball, bogmen with balls, and chains tied down around their ankles, these are their anklets, innocent gang fighting for justice, "The righteous are bold", sometime in the future all the bogs in the country will be used up. There will be no more turf left, we'll fight for it while we're in it man, until we take the last breath, this part of Irish country life is very deep, not to be under- estimated, it is part of our whole being, don't mess with it."

Turf war, tough battle, taking the compesation and free trailers of turf, delivered to your back yard, might be an easier and wiser option. Twist of fate, the Summer of 2012 was a complete and total wash-out, not much turf saved here lads, it all back-fired big-time. Ye got drenched in the trenches of war.

"Not at all, this is all about principles, if a man or indeed a woman hasn't principles they have nothing. It's standing up to Brussels bureaucracy gone crazy, outrageous bullying with brain power. We're retaliating with muscle power, standing up, being counted, fighting strongly, idiots at the top have miscalculated. They're in a match here, "Fortunes favour the brave", government up to their makers are trying to savage the soul out of rural Ireland and wipe it out, cop on, for Pete's sake, because the bog-men and turf-cutters aren't goin' to back down, they're goin' to stand their ground.

We are the total and complete owners of our bog-land, and frankly it's not for sale, it's ours and we want to keep it and work it, it is basic human rights. It's simple locgic, they'll never buy us out. The Hell-icopters are back, this was supposed to be part of the roar of the Celtic Tiger. What a waste of tax-payers' money. Are Governments in this country ever going to learn? That's it in a nut-shell, too much monkey business, once again they're shooting themselves in the nuts."

Padraic Reaney

At the core of every human being there is a very dangerous animal. This is there because men and women descended from the animals as we all know. Most people never release this outrageous monster and this keeps them human. **– Padraic Reaney**

Radiation And Its Consequences

1. Radiation – What is it?
2. Health Risks
3. The Chernobyl Accident
4. Sellafield
5. Nuclear Disarmanent
6. Its use in the treatment of illnesses. (Such as Cancer)

1. Radiation – What is it?

Radiation is energy that travels and spreads out as it goes. Visible light that comes from a lamp in your house or radio waves that come from a radio station are the two types of electromagnetic radiation. Radiation means energy in the form of electromagnetic waves of acoustical waves. The Electromagnetic Spectrum (EM) is a name given to various types of radiation. There is radiation from computer monitors' and microwave ovens, and there is also radiation from mobile phones which can be dangerous.

2. Health Risks

The toxiecity of low-level radioactive fallout is responsible for distinct and consistent increases in mortality rates as well as cancers, leukemia, birth defects and rises in chronic diseases. For instance in Chernobyl, 125,000 people alone have died, from diseases related to the accident, according to the Ukraine's Health Ministry. Also, about 7,000 people in the Chernobyl who helped put out the fire and seal the reactor are believed to have died and 38% are recovering from some kind of disease.

Plutonium is a highly toxic metallic transuranic element. It occurs in trace amounts in uranium ores and is produced in a nuclear reactor by neutron bombardment of uranium-238. The most stable isotope plutonium-239, readily undergoes fission and is used as a reactor fuel, and it has a half-life of 24,360 years. The planet Pluto lies beyond Neptune and plutonium was discovered soon after Neptune.

The most prevalent form of radiation plutonium emits is alpha radiation. Then alpha particles could damage a person's lungs. This damage would typically show up as cancer after a period of years. Plutonium can also be dangerous if it gets into the blood stream. The most likely way for plutonium to get into the blood stream is through an open wound. If this occured it would tend to concentrate in bones. If enough plutonium were to get to the bones, the alpha radiation could harm the bone-marrow. This could cause leukemia or other bone-marrow related problems.

3. The Chernobyl Accident

The largest ever radiation accident involving a nuclear reactor occured on the 26th of April 1986 at the Chernobyl nuclear power plant in the Ukraine of which there was heavy contamination. Tens of thousands of people have died as a result. A high percentage suffer from some kind of disease also. Ivan Kenik, Belarus's Chernobyl minister, estimated the cost within the borders of Belarus for "total damages from the Chernobyl catastrophe from 1986 to 2015" to be $235 billion.

Chernobyl is the clearest single message to humanity that Nuclear Technology is not an appropriate exercise of human intelligence. But despite this Russia plans a Nuclear Renaissance.

Russia will build at least 4 nuclear reators at home and others in China, Iran, India and ex-Soviet republics as parr of an ambitious plan to revive the atomic industry after the severe shock caused by the 1986 Chernobyl disaster. The Nuclear ministry is considering plans to complete another two nuclear reators in the Ukraine, and another in the ex-Soviet Republic of Kazakstan.

4. Sellafield

A week before Christmas in 2001 Sellafield in England got a lot of news coverage, on account of the opening of the controversial MOX nuclear reprocessing plant, on Thursday 20th Dec. The Irish government launched a last ditch legal bid to try to halt the opening of the MOX nuclear plant in Sellafield on that day. The move came after it emerged that several reactors were closed at the nuclear facility without the Irish government being informed in line with stated agreements.

Junior minister Joe Jacob, responsible for nuclear safety, said the government presented what he called "its substantive case" against MOX to the International Tribunal of the Law of the Sea. The Tribunal's 21 judges who claim jurisdiction in the case ruled earlier that month that the UK must share information with Ireland about the £475m plant, and Mr. Jacob said, "The MOX opening was an act of supreme arrogance." Demonstrators, including some Irish politicians, gathered outside the complex in protest.

5. Nuclear Disarmanent

The British grassroots organisation engage in campaigns against nuclear weapon. CNN campaigns non-violently to rid the world of nuclear weapons and other Weapons of mass destruction and to create genuine security for future generations.

Its aims are:To change government policies to bring about the elimination of British nuclear weapon as a major contribution to global abolition. To stimulate wide public debate on the need for alternatives both to the nuclear cycle and to the military attempts to resolve conflict.To empower people to engage actively in the political process and to work for a nuclear-free and peaceful future.

A British nuclear-powered Trident submarine is on patrol ready, 24 hours a day, 365 days a year, to fire sixteen nuclear-armed missiles. Each submarine carries 48 independently-targeted nuclear warheads. Each warhead has seven times the explosive power of the first atomic bomb. The atomic bomb that was dropped on the Japanese city of Hiroshima, killing 140,000 civilians. It costs Britain L1.5 billion every year.

6.Its use in the treatment of illnesses. (Such as Cancer)

The atom bomb explosions Hiroshima and Nagasaki produced fresh evidence incriminating high doses of radiation as a cancer-producing agent. A very high incidence of leukaemia was found in survivors who were close the the explosions, and the higher the radiation dose from the bomb the greater the likelihood of their developing the disease.

In contrast to a biological cause of cancer we now turn to a physical agent that is capable, under certain special circumstances, of producing a cancerous change. This is atomic radiation. It is a valuable tool which is being used increasingly in everyday life. Not only is it used in the X-ray departments of hospitals but radioactive isotopes (which are substances producing radiation) are playing an important part in treatment and research. In many industrial processes, radioactive isotopes and X-rays are used.

Radiations (in the form of X-rays) were first discovered by Rontgen in1895. Rontgen could have little idea of the great impact this discovery was to have in the field of cancer alone. For not only does it constitute one of the main methods of treatment but it is invaluable for diagnosis. This is especially so in the case of lung cancer.

Conclusion:

England has announced recently that it will have anoteher nuclear power station by the year 2023. Albert Einstein's theory of relativiy, $E=mc2$, expressing the equivalence between matter and energy. This has also been tested experimentally, rather too often, because it is the principle behind the explosion of atomic bombs. The public responded to Einstein with unqualified admiration, but Big Science later gave the world nuclear weapons.

World leaders should show restraint when faced with International conflict. Some peple may remember one week in October 1962 – The Cuban Missile Crisis – when the world watched tensely as the U.S. and the Soviet Union seemed poised to go to war. We should all learn form the past.

Man should have more intelligence than to destroy himself, Nuclear War ... Armageddon?

Kieran Reaney

Chris Toledo is seen here at the Vatican presenting his portrait of the late Pope John Paul II, who held a private audience with the artists whilst they were in Rome for an international Mouth and Foot Painting Artists meeting. With his arms and feet paralysed from birth, Chris particularly enjoys landscape painting in oils. Pope John Paul II visited Ireland in late September, early October 1979.
Photo courtesy of MFPA, Pineview, Firhouse Road, Dublin 16.

In this life the person that never experienced a huge amount of pain and suffering never learned anything about life. – **Padraic Reaney.**

No Pope, No Hope

Titanic, Centenary celebrations 2012.
Famous for all the wrong reasons.
If it had stayed up, it wouldn't have got
As much publicity, this is man's twisted soul.

People love tha bad, negative story, it's a fact.
My grand-parents, decades ago,
Told an enthusiastic tale of this 'unsinkable ship'.
Some sharp, observant person was drawn,

To lettering displayed somewhere on the huge
Liner – which had class distinction for passengers –
When this individual played around,
With the letters in their head.

They could see "No Pope" in it, a recipe for,
Failure, doomed, desperate disaster, set sail in the

Name of satan, evil devil, now over a century later,
Rotting in the bowels of hell

Padraic Reaney

Honest to God: Since the recession came volunteerism in community development has turned fully professional, but community development is on a downward trend. A lot of people always got paid for the work they did, and ironically 'backbenchers' who did little or no work, and might be as well off on the high-stool, always kept an eye on 'the kitty'. **– Kieran Reaney.**

Doctor's Orders

Paddy Joe and Louise were going out together for only six months when everyone were shocked at the announcement of their wedding. Paddy Joe was a quiet, respectable man, a farmer in his early forties. He was an honest man but he wasn't the sharpest tool in the tool-shed in relation to girls, and his cat often got caught in the moustrap. Louise was 29, frisky and streetwise, and she had been around the block a few times.

On their wedding night they decided they would stay in Paddy Joe's house, and for the next couple of weeks tour Ireland. On the morning after the wedding, Paddy Joe got out of the bed without any clothes on, and walked towards the window and opened the curtains. "Come away from that window fast or the neighbours' will think I married you for your money," said Louise.

A few weeks went by and even though Paddy Joe seemed to be happy enough, Louise wasn't. Things began to annoy her quite easily, especially night-time activity or lack of it. One day Paddy Joe was trying to pump the front tyre of the tractor as Louise looked on. A woman from next door walked into the yard and said, "Is she flat again?" "Oh! Hello, Mrs. Donaghy," said Paddy Joe. Mrs. Donaghy's husband worked in town during the week, and they had a bit of land as well, so she was well used to wearing the long pants as well as the short pants. "Where's the nipple key?" said Mrs. Donaghy, "You need the nipple key to open the valve or you'll never jump it."

Paddy Joe went into the shed to try to find the nipple key, and Mrs. Donaghy gave Louise a little elbow and said, "He's doin' all-right, is he?" "Ah!" said Louise, "He's so innocent he would think a black suspender was a Jamaican hangman", and she continued, "Or that a man working in a bra factory was making hats for Siamese twins!" They both had a good auld laugh, even though Louise hadn't laughed that much in recent times, and had suggested that herself and Paddy Joe should see a doctor.

That evening as they were about to go to town to do the shopping the car wouldn't start, and Paddy Joe thought Louise would give it a bit of a push. "What do you think I am?" Louise in an angry tone of voice, "I'll get Mrs. Donaghy's young lad with the jump leads, he'll do it, and it's about time you got a new battery." On their way home from shopping Louise got in bd form again and said, "We'll see the doctor after dinner tomorrow."

The doctor was listening attentively and fidding with his pen ready to write a prescription, when all of a sudden he seemed to get a bid of inspiration, "Take off all your clothes there, Louise," said the doctor, and she did, and then he said, "Lie up there on the couch." The doctor then made mad, passionate love with Louise, and then he sat on the side of the couch. He starting counting on the fingers of one hand and he said, "She would want that now, Monday night, Tuesday night, Thursday night, Friday night and Saturday night." Paddy Joe looked at the doctor and he said, "Will I bring her in to see you or will you call out yourself, doctor?"

Kieran Reaney

In rural Ireland in the 1950s a girl dancing at the crossroads might have a name called Lucy Pender. At the present time a girl dancing at the crossroads would be called 'loose suspender'. **–Kieran Reaney.**

Hackett's Castle at the foot of Knockma Hill.

Lovers

Through wood and meadow,
And running streams low.
Over hill and hollow,
Driving rain and snow.

Like a fox ensnared,
Hearts curled and dared.
A moon hath stared,
On hibernating, warmth cared.

Biting dandelions, the pail,
The dust and flail.
Excruciating cries and wail,
The lost beagles derail.

Petticoat and red dress,
The hounds of recess.
Bushy hair, tangled stress,
Dying pain, no caress.

Kieran Reaney

Prosaic poetry can never be a masterpiece. – **Kieran Reaney.**

No Pullet

A Galway farmer with hair like Ruud Gullit.
Goes on a long trip after birds to Belmullet.
He says, "For the Green and Red I'll cheer."
They say, "You'll get no fun here."
And eventually they give him the bullet!

Kieran Reaney

Teddy Boy: An easy going lad will blow into his girlfriend's porridge in the morning, but she will never blow his porridge. – **Kieran Reaney.**

Victims

With this recession ...
Romantics, soft hearts.
Love hearts, pussy cats.
Dreamers, believers.
Soft-centred toffees.

Weepies, Valentine's Day cards.
Cry babies, Christmas cheer.
Christmas tree, decorations.
"God bless the work."
Wish them good luck.
Put out the hand.
Congratulate the man.

Passionate men.
Men of vision.
Patriots, never-say-die.
Heart and soul.
Visitors, hearts of gold.
Gentle giants, country meitheal.
Are a dying breed.

Kieran Reaney.

The beauty of democracy is a person has a right to abstain or not to vote. The only way to unnerve a politician is the whole electorate not to vote. – **Kieran Reaney**

The Nature Of Things

In rural Ireland in the 1950s there was a great character called Micilín Mór. He was almost forty-five years old and very tall, very quiet and calm, but he was also very sly. He would peel an orange in his pocket, but he didn't drink and the bicycle was his only means of transport, as indeed it was for a lot of people in those days.

One cold Sunday night in the depths of winter he was cycling to a dance in the Parish Hall. When he arrived he was carefully placing his bicycle against the wall outside and was putting a plastic bag over the saddle, in case it rained. Suddenly four lads, after having a few drinks in the local pub, were cycling towards him, and one of then said, "There'll be no rain tonight, Micilín." Another lad said, "I'm telling ye now lads, bring the bicycle pumps into the cloakroom and leave them with the coats. They won't last a minute on the bikes until they'll be gone."

Just then Micilín went behind the hall. "Where's he gone?" the third lad said. There was a quick reply, "He's gone to drain the spuds!" The four lads burst out laughing. Another one of them said, "Sure no-one would go any place now without a bell on their bike," and continued, "Who was that wan you were carrying on the bar of that bike the last night?" The lad replied, "Molly Gilhooley." The lad that asked the question said, "Ye wouldn't get pulled by a guard for no light anyway." A question followed, "How do you make that out?" A quick response was, " Because she has a fine set of headlamps!"

When Micilín came back the four lads had gon and he went into the dance on his own. He decided inside that he would leave his overcoat on as it was really cold. The atmosphere was so bad it was reminiscent of a geriatric ward. He spotted two attractive girls sipping their soft drinks, he noticed another girl standing on her own, a bit over to the right, Abigail Kirrane.

She wasn't that streetwise, a bit of a prude and quite cranky, but she would enjoy a simple joke or two when she would thaw out. You wouldn't shift her with a Hy-Mac and she was harder to get at than Fort Knox. Local lads thought she was from Hackballscross in County Louth. Everyone knew that Abigail in relation to lucky stars wasn't a Sagittarious, 'twould be more like a Virgo. She was like a bobsleigh, you would have to run after her first and then jump on her.

But Micilín thought he would get a dance anyway and besides 'a bird in the hand is worth two with thrush'. In gentlemanly tye of way he put out his hand and said, "Can I have the pleasure of this dance, Abigail?" But to his amazement her reply was, "What sort a pleasure?" in a cross tone of voice. Micilín then said, Ye got a good price for the cattle last week." Abigail then got in good form and said, "Come on" and walked to the centre of the hall, Micilín followed.

Micilín was so stiff and tight in the muscles you would want 3-in-1 oil to loosen him up. As they say, "A lot of body parts work much better when they're lubricated." The band were playing a slow waltz and Abigail got very close to Micilín. "I see you have the bicycle pump inside your overcoat," said Abigail. "'Tis to be sure," said Micilín. The waltz ended and Micilín asked could he see her again, and she said that she would be there the following Sunday night, but she would be half an hour late, as she had to visit someone whose husband had passed away recently. She asked was that all right, and Micilín replied, "'Tis to be sure."

At the end of the night as Micilín was walking outside the hall, a lad came up behind him and said, "You son of a gun, Micilín the bicycle pump is still there." "'Tis to be sure," said Micilín, as he threw a leg on the bike and off he went.

Kieran Reaney

It runs in the family: An idiosyncrasy that a person may have could also have been the idosyncrassy of that person's parents, grand-parents, great grand-parents or even further back, on either side. – **Padraic Reaney.**

Saddle Sore

The only eroticism in Ireland in the early 1970s – apart from in the cinemas, where soft porn films were shown at that time – was the Christmas Circus and Womens' Tennis, obviously on a windy day! Take your time, lads, steady up, no rush, it's not an Olympic Sport! There's no prize fot being first. In fact it's like the slow bicycle race, the lad that finishes last is the winner! The impatient lad always misses desert. No drugs now, lads!

Padraic Reaney

A man heed to politicians and a man going to a call girl end up with exactly the same thing: they both get screwed. – **Padraic Reaney.**

The Middle Man Deserted

Celtic Tiger roaring,
Cute Auctioneer glowing.
Substantial amount of
Money made, bills paid.

Thinking about going to 'Americay',
Goodbye Galway Bay.
Mansion in Beverly Hills,
A retired couple's thrills.

The booming economy went bust,
So did his wife's lust.
Marriage no longer got out of
The blocks, scotch on the rocks.

It all fell apart,
He took it very hard.
To save money everyone ran,
And by-passed the Middle Man.

Padraic Reaney

There are only tow extreme types of insanity: Insane with sanity and insane with insanity. – **Padraic Reaney.**

Ye're All Stone Mad

Third Level College, most students taking it very seriously. Studying hard, not much light-hearted activity. All work and no play ... makes a person a Jack ass. In life the arse-licker usually ends up getting their own arse kicked. Jack was as happy as a clown, but ironically the loneliest man in the Circus. But no-one could say that he had no spirit. He was obsessed with tennis, and played it at every opportunity. He would go crazy and cracked, in different college situations, for up to half an hour at a time. Then he would let fly small pebbles, that he had collected the previous day, at lighting speed onto a nearby wall. Lots of his friends were endeavouring to be steady, and thought that he was nuts. He would say, "Ye're all stome mad." Which begs the question, "What's natural and normal? What's sane and insane? Who can say it? Who knows it? Was it the method of his madness, if he was mad? Now he's a very successful middle-aged business man. Game, set and match!

Padraic Reaney

If a person does well, a lot of people are reluctant to 'put out the hand' but love to throw the punch. – **Kieran Reaney.**

Abbeytown Cemetery

Learn how to bargain in life, because towards the end of your life, you will be bargaining with God to give you more time. – **Padraic Reaney.**

Epitaph

Excessive drinker, chickened out.
White feather, lost his head.
Drugs, Head shops, stoned, head-stoned.
Footlose, footless, headless, gone down.

Padraic Reaney

In real life there are no time-outs. – **Padraic Reaney.**

Almost Perfect

Red car, door and toenails.
Circling around, inside and wails.
Walking on the corridor lit.
The paws kiss the carpet.

The coarse tongue licks.
The coarse shaven armpits.
The unshaven, tired whiskers.
A game for riskers.

Black cat and hair.
Of a temporary affair.
Threading over pierced navel.
Gentle claws are unable.

In a time from afar.
Lays the tummy's blemished scar.
Where once kitten came.
Succumbed to temptation, don't blame.

Dying to see her again.
In life does anyone win?
Opening the door I departed.
Inside she stood there, naked.

Kieran Reaney

Neither male nor female people are monogamous. – **Kieran Reaney.**

Clais An Aifrinn, Sylane.   *The Altar and Cross date back to 1680.*

Mass Rocks, Hedge Schools And Milestones

Mass Rocks: In the 18th century the cruel Penal Laws were passed in Ireland. Priests' and Bishops were not allowed to say Mass. The people gathered together in the open at Mass Rocks, which sometimes were down in a hollow part of a field and surrounded by trees. While the Priest said Mass someone was on guard keeping a lookout.

Hedge Rocks: In Ireland Catholic schools were forbidden under the Penal Laws from 1723 to 1782. Secret schools known as hedge schools were set up for the Catholic children. These were called 'scoileanna scairte' in Irish. Most of the teachers were men although there were women teachers as well. The teacher would sit under a tree which had a hedgerow nearby and was a quiet place like in a wood. The education varied from school to school, mostly reading, writing and arithmetic were taught. Some children were very young, but others were as old as 18 or 19 and were taught Latin and Greek.

Milestones: From Mossfort in Caherlistrane, the 7 miles to Tuam by the Weir road, was marked by milestones. There were fairly big numbers, carved onto a rectangular solid stone and built into the wall on the right hand side of the road, from the Mossfort side. In the late 60s and early 70s most of them were still to be seen, but for years back most of the wall is gone and some is now covered by ivy. There was one across the road from Sylane Hurling Club and one near Donnellan's house.

Kieran Reaney

Late Sixties

In '69 I was only six.
My first time between the sticks.
"Watch the ball." The swirling flight.
The wood denies, out of sight.

The exciting flair and the dash.
The peaceful wood and the ash.
Dreams of a long football career.
God's blessing of an unanswered prayer.

The Woodstock year, didn't know then.
Yasgur's farm, would it all begin?
Years later walking through the wood.
Where alfred and Tinseltown stood.

Dad carried me on the bike.
Going to town I did like.
They were golden carefree times.
Quiet roads and Church bell chimes.

Strolling the streets through the town.
The cinema matinée, credits roll down.
Broken chariot wheel, now a blur.
St. Jarlath's town and Ben Hur.

The yellow daffodils and May flower.
Fair hair curls from Round Tower.
Clais An Aifrinn and the Milestones.
The lemonade and ice cream cones.

Circus in the Fair Green and trapeze.
Walking on the moon with ease.
The Fleadh Ceoil and monochrome TV.
This era, ne'er again we'll see.

Kieran Reaney

Positive publicity and anonymity are both sweet, and only by a lot of experience of one does a person realise the real sweetness of the other. – **Kieran Reaney.**

How're Ya Doin' Sham?

Green Shamrock Bar,
Babysham, Sham-Rock,
Shamtown, Red Stars.

Padraic Reaney

Anyone that doesn't get caught, especially if they do the catching, will never get bitter. – **Kieran Reany.**

Tuam Remembered

1970s, cold, frosty, refreshing Winters.
Five Secondary Schools, bee-line for girls.
Sugar Factory smoking, beet campaign swinging.
Pubs overflowing, traditional music, alcohol singing.

Blaze X igniting, The Sex Pistols blasting it out
Across the pond, rockin' around the clock.
Sweet night-shift. Las Vegas at the hop.
Dancers left with lost wages, loving slow skates.

Trains rattling by, easy-going, everything on track.
Ice cool, railway of un-ending happiness.
Groovy Grove Hospital booming. Peaceful,
Easy Feeling. Mart's mid-night mooing.

Hot films showing in cinemas. Bingo-goers
Excited, brave political warriors, Hunger Strike,
Bread and butter issues. Basketball players,
A thirst for success, Galway lock horns with

"The Dubs" in the Stadium, home of Maroon
And White football, blissful hunting ground
For The Tribesmen, charge of the light-blue
Brigade reversed, "Tuam was once the seat of

The High King of Ireland, Sham",
Comaraderie. Atmosphere, mighty craic and
Joy in abundance, they were good oul' days,
In many ways, and great times.

Padraic Reaney

When a lad is young and going to college, when he goes to the cupboard it is bare, after getting married he is afraid of skeletons in the cupboard, and when he is getting old he wants to hide in the cupboard. **– Kieran Reaney.**

Having Your Cake Or Eating It

Some people get too much of it,
Other people don't get enough of it,
Some people can't get enough of it,
People that nevert got it,

Don't know what they're missing,
How could they when they never got it,
But these people really got it,
If they got it they may not like it,

One man's meat, another woman's poison,
One woman's meat, another man's poison,
By the way did you get it?
Chocolate gateaux I'm talking about!

Padraic Reaney

With a girl a man is hardly ever the first and never the only one. **– Kieran Reaney.**

The Person That Laughs Last Laughs Most

A husband is driving his wife crazy by his actions. She is constantly nagging him, criticising him big time. When he smokes cigarettes or cigars it gets on her nerves. She says that he has more tar inside him than would resurface all the roads in County Galway. He replies with no concern, "Sure it's only a habit."

When he drinks alcohol she complains immediately. She tells her friends that he has a drinking problem. They laughed and say, "He has no problem at all drinking, stopping is the problem!" He says, "Sure it's only a habit."

When he takes prescribed drugs she says that he is 'a pharmaceutical junkie'. He replies calmly, "Sure it's only a habit." When he takes hard drugs, she says that he has seen more 'white poweder' than some women see talcum powder, and stuck more needles into himself than you'd see in a tailor's shop. He says cooly, "Peace woman, it's only a habit."

While out one night in a pub, drinking with the lads, a funny barman told a risqué or maybe risky joke. "Did ye hear about the hundred Nuns who were cycling very happily around the Convent grounds on bicycles, moaning and groaning and enjoying themselves immensely." There wa a golden silence. Then the barman continued, "A hefty Mother Superior rushed out the door and said, "If ye don't quieten down girls, and stop making such a racket, I'll have no option but to put the saddles back on the bicycles."

They all went cracked with laughter and he had got an idea for spicing things up in the bedroom. He stored it inside his head, and after about a week later, after coming home from the pub, he decided to play it out. It was around three o'clock in the morning, he was feelin' mad randy, and he went into the bedroom dressed up entirely in a Nun's outfit.

He switched on the light and his wife woke up suddenly. With a broad smile on his face he said confidently, "I amn't wearing a thing underneath." She wasn't impressed or interested and she replied in a drowsy tone of voice, "Ah! Sure it's only a habit!"

Padraic Reaney

Using his head: When a man is young, he talks with one head and thinks with two heads. As he reaches middle age, and gets wiser and more mature, he talks with one head, and thinks with one head. If he is lucky enough to reach old age, he loses both heads, I'm not sure in which order. – **Kieran Reaney.**

Played Puck

Roman Catholic Church, Tricolour,
Church and State, strict, hypocritical regimes
Of exorbitant, extravagant conservatism.
A country riddled with Institutions.
Watchdogs of morality, or lack of,
Ironically, preaching, barking,
One thing, practising another.

People horrified, outraged, all
Types of sick, evil abuse.
They didn't do themselves any favours.
Who could take them seriously again?
Believe in them, pay heed to them or trust them.
Eventually when they were pushed

Out or jumped ship, the Government
Began to have a field day, everyday.
Hectares of space in fact,

All hell broke loose, no control,
Spiralling, gaining momentum,
Not nipped in the bud, like an old, withered,
Weather-beaten, dying flower.
The once clear, bright, distinctive
Green, White and Gold,
Perished, hungry for leadership
And with no direction, as it slowly
Began to fade into oblivion.

Padraic Reaney

The people that are in most with God are tempted the most. The bad people are already caught by satan. – Padraic Reaney.

Lost Maiden

Over the mountain she did come.
The fair-haired maiden, the orchards plum.
The vesseled leaves, the heartstrings undone.
Kissed her thrice, and did run.

Through fledgling fields, and summer's sun.
Shed novice dreams, frolics and fun.
The ice cracked, startling and spun.
Another world, aching hearts, forever won.

Silver threads, reminisce the memories numb.
The outstretched hand, where fingers begun.
The circled ice, it did shun.
The fire-quenched thirst of soothing rum.

Kieran Reaney

From Learner Driver To Full Throttle

Eamon De Valera, worried, new television station.
Doors opened, new approach to Irish life.
Shackles of strict conservatism extinguished,
Left for dead. Paddy throws off the oul' L plates.
Caution to the wind, full steam ahead.

Ireland joins European Economic Community.
We're livin' in the dark ages man, get in with
Europe, get a soft few bob,
Whatever other perks 'come' with it.
Hot newspapers, now Paddy reads between
The legs instead of between the lines.
Soft porn films shown in Cinemas.
Ireland could not handle Art class nudity.
Ironically in the same year, 1978, the
Video recorder became available.

For Paddy it was like letting loose
A young boy in a sweet-shop.
Ahops renting out video tapes, DVDs all over
The country, new lease of life for Paddy.
Sex, violece, horror, the 'big three' sellers.

You won't be able to play the accordion,
After it, Paddy maybe dance the Hornpipe.
Multi-channel TV, deflector systems,
Erotic thrillers, satellite systems dishing
Out pornography, controversy on a plate.

Any censorship? Seemingly anything
And everything goes. Paddy always longed
To be the fly on the wall, close-up and personal.
Now he could be the flea in the bed, bravo.
Celtic Tiger era accompanied by small

Sexual revolution, evolution. Playboy magazine
Legalised, flood gates open for other X-rated,
Explicit publications. Sex, shops, prostitution
Takes off, becomes widespread, dogging sites,
Decadence. Brothels, massage parlours, call girls.

Escort agencies, exotic lap dancing clubs, letting
It rip. Computers, internet, w.w.w.,
World wide web, mad, bad, sick, evil material
Available here. A black deadly spider, carefully
And intricately weaving his 'quick sand' tapestry. No

Way out web, satan planning world wide destruction,
Annihilation, be scrupulous here, tread carefully.

Padraic Reaney

A person after passing the driving test then get back to the way they usually drive.
- Kieran Reaney.

Galway's Dream

On the 9th day in September
In the year of 2012.
Galway drew with the Black and Amber.
And left Liam McCarthy waiting on the shelf.

O'er the mountains and the hills.
The robin and the lark.
The excitement and the thrills.
Of Galway hurlers' in Croke Park.

For 24 years we have waited.
Like children building castles on the sand.
The Maroon and White waves have stated.
Galway may reach the Promised Land.

With gallant captain Fergal Moore.
Fullback Kevin Hynes and James Skehill in the goal.
Niall Donohue and Tony Óg Regan were secure.
The swiftness of David Collins and Johnny Coen.

Trojan midfielders Iarla Tannian and Andy Smith.
Cyril Donnellan, Niall Burke and Damien Hayse.
The Cats were clawing bit by bit.
But were left in daze.

Saviour Joe Canning, James Regan and David Burke.
The Cooney's, David Glennon and Jonathan Glynn.
Still remaining seventy minutes of hard work.
For these lion-hearted Galway men.

If Galway wins the play.
Galway city will see many a traffic jam.
Infinite words of praise on Galway Bay.
For the quiet and modest, Anthony Cunningham.

Galway hurling we salute you.
Scenes of joy and happiness.

Hopefully the Liam McCarthy will come home anew.
To our beloved Galway in the West.

Kieran Reaney

Above poem was written after Galway's draw with Kilkenny in the All- Ireland Senior Hurling Championship final in September 2012 and before the replay. Congratulations to Gillian O'Connor (Caherlistrane), and the Galway Senior Ladies football team who put two Connacht titles back-to-back last summer. Also, the Galway Minor girls who won the All-Ireland Minor Football Championship final.

Life is not what you make it, it's what you have to live it. **-Kieran Reaney.**

Christy O'Connor's *award winning book The Club which tells about the G.A.A. openly and frankly. Christy is a brother of the great Clare hurler Jamesie O'Connor.*

July Sunday

It's a long, long way.
To Semple Stadium next Sunday.
The Tribesmen and the banter.
Will they lower the Banner?

From Ennis to Milltown Malbay.
Near Oranmore and Galway Bay.
The hurleys they will fly.
Old hurlers in the sky.

Both teams they will play.
The passion and the clay.
Hope the better team wins.
Shake hands, two neighbouring friends.

Kieran Reaney

This poem was written a few days before Galway and Clare Senior hurlers played in the Championship in Semple Stadium this year.

Liberalism Blazing

Extreme, maybe at times damaging,
Laws, rules and regulations of
Strict conservatism, maybe old-fashioned,
Out-dated, changed to soul-destroying,

Killer, anything and everything seemingly
Allowed, accepted, free and easy, devastating,
Radical humanitarianism. Innocent Ireland
Of the past, old school of thought.

Middle Ages, Roman Catholic Church,
Rock heavy influences, powerless fish caught,
Entangled in no escape route, no way out
Of outrageous, brain-washing manipulation.

Solid stone cracked, blown to pieces
By dynamite of sick corruption, exploding,
Blackening the soul of authority.

Fish run riot, or maybe wrong.

Like mice at cross-road,
Where's the big, fat, cute cat hiding?
Fish-net stockings, sweet twettie bird
Teasing, flirting, part of Eve in every woman,

Part of Adam in every man,
He can resist anything but temptation.
Too late for him to say that he
Prefers pears now, pairs surely, he surrendered

Tamely, without losing a white feather,
Irish society destroyed, never to be the same,
Modern Eire caught, tied up, gone down in satan's
Laughing net, scorched soul on dirt track to hell.

Eventually sooty chimney leads
To out of control sulfur furnace,
Never smoke without fire, maybe brimstone?
Is it gone too far to start closing the damper?

Padraic Reaney

A promiscuous girl, if she isn't married in her thirties, tries to snare an innocent lad who would run to the altar. All the lads she slept with up until that never wanted to hear about marriage, and would be reluctant to have a bit of fun again with her even if given a chance. -**Kieran Reaney.**

Destiny

The clamour shrilled for days and daze.
The barrels filled, wept tears and haze.
Swept the sweat of back and gaze.
Mirror of cobwebs and fog ne'er erase.

The hair-tunnelled hand, it did amaze.
Tucked in paws, the cat did laze.
The Sphinx demise, the decades my maze.
Cruel fate denies, the hearts ablaze.

Kieran Reaney

Avoiding Atheism

In Ireland, or indeed any country in the world, at any given time, if the people at the top, the Government, the law-makers or whoever, continue to peel off more layers of the onion liberalism, this eventually leads to disillusionment, confusion and total chaos, because ultimately you're left with nothing. Everything is destroyed, from ethical and morality points of view, and the mud-slide of disaster slowly slips down the mountain-side, and into the bowels of oblivion. By taking the route a country is in the road to hell.

Some people might say that in Ireland, due to the fact that many of these vitality important issues, are decided by referenda, which is the voice of the people, or democracy in action, it is totally above board. This point is accepted by me, but my other point is, do some of the people, really know what exactly they're voting for, and most important of all, what implications these decisions may have, five or ten years in the future, obviously if they win in the various referenda. In many of these situations, the arguments for both sides are very well presented, and when all the pros and cons are weighed up, it's six to one, one side and half a dozen to one the other. If in doubt, stay out because some of these choices may have huge side-effects, sooner or later. In any society, there has to be laws, rules and regulations, but if they are continuously being relaxed, the whole scenario begins to become opened up, and lowers itself to the law of the jungle scheme.

During the last century, the 20th. Century the Russian people learned this the hard way, as they have endured for many decades, enforced state atheism, which still continues. This has led to alcoholism, drug-taking, high crime rates, huge immorality and all types of corruption. The spirit and enthusiasm of the people has been damaged enormously and is terribly low. They are now turning to drink, drugs, and occultism to fill their spiritual emptiness, instead of God, religious beliefs and convictions, and staying on the straight and narrow. But having said that, it is a known fact that the human being – both male and female – are pleasure seeking animals, and also very much into social contact.

However, the basis of most religions is probably taking the pain, no pain-no gain mentality, or in other words, not running to the pub every minute. In Russia since 1939, Catholic priests have all been eliminated and all of their seminaries closed. In their country the people are consequently searching desperately for faith and belief in God, for inspirational spirituality and the associated and well connected to this, meaning of life. Some people may think atheism is freedom but on close analysis it's nonsensical and insane and is definitely the evil work of satan. As they say if you don't believe in something, you'll fall for anything. Not believing in anything is deadly.

In Ireland they should learn from Russia's predicament and not get caught in a similar excruciatingly painful trap. The brutal, soul-destroying unhappiness of a country torn apart by corruption and strict austerity, much of it aimed at insecure, vulnerable and poverty-stricken people, of a land not at peace or unity with itself is like a time-bomb ready to explode. As they say everyone has a breaking point, and when people are pushed to the limit, especially due to outrageous unfairness, they have a tendency to rebel.

Padraic Reaney

In recent months, for the very first time in the 213 year history of St. Jarlath's College, in Tuam, the President or Principal position is a lay teacher, and not a Priest. We all wish John Kelly, from Louisburgh, Co. Mayo, all the very best in this prestigious position. **–Kieran and Padraic Reaney.**

Food For Thought: *Old Russian woman eating soup to nourish her body but hungry and heartbroken for a deep spiritual meaning.*

Reading Between The Wrinkles

Around forty years old, ripening maturity.
Seeing a photograph of my great grand-mother.
In her old age, for the very first time.
My mind's eye saw her, keeping it together

With dignity. Looking calm, like a duck,
But paddling crazily beneath the surface.
Hiding behind the pain, hurt and often terrible
Heartbreak. Mother of a large family, not much

Work less money, small house, hard to make
Ends meet, inevitable emigration. Shores Of
Americay for most of them, nothing at home.
Outskirts of Tuam town, an ambulance speeds by.
Sirens blaring, her daughter says to woman
Beside her," Unfortunately trouble for some

Unlucky family there." It was her own husband
In that ambulance, but she never knew it.

He got very badly burned in an accident in the
Sugar Factory and eventually died from the injuries
He sustained. Sweet times had turned sour.
Her grandson experienced the atrocities of war in

Korea. Then looking much deeper into the sad
And lonely windows of her soul, years and decades
Earlier, my third eye saw, Famine times,
Outrageous hunger, starvation, tortured suffering.

Black 1847, young girl on the streets in
Galway city, desperately trying to find a morsel
Of marrow on a dog's bone. Poor with poverty,
Rich in spirit, never room at the Inn of the nice,

Good and righteous. God began calling her,
She walked slowly, energetically drained,
Yet enthusiastic, suddenly she could hear
Amazing Grace being sung by beautiful Angels.

Wild Atlantic waves' lashing, who has sinned?
Who'll throw the first stone? Cuchulainn giants,
Maroon and White sliotar missiles navigating,
On target, pin-point accuracy, old Cladagh

Women, dressed in black, head-to-toe, Galway
Shawls, fishermen, fishers of men, drinking
Glasseens of stout and smoking clay pipes,
Stout-hearted Connemara men, just like in

Gallilee, Shining Brendan singing The Nazireen.
And she could see Lough Corrib over-flowing
With soup. But she no longer needed it.
Then a magical avenue was opened up across

This nutritious lake, and she walked ecstatically
And euphorically across it to the other side,
Across the great divide, she was saved,
And tears of broth rolled down my face.

My poignant drops erupted into a lovely sight

Beautiful girls dancing at a cross-road.
Glamorous Goddesses, chicks with sticks.
West awakening, loud, passionate shouts.
"Tá Craobh na h-Éireann ar ais i nGaillimh."

Padraic Reaney

In this world no-one flies through life, a small minority may fly through a short spell, which only lasts a few hours. After that a person's mood changes, or another person or people knock you off your high horse. – **Kieran Reaney.**

Our Lady's Holy Well in Kilcoona.

Getting Old

The Summer hath gone, lays the winter beyond.
The eyes are filled, and rivers are swelled.
Now on the hill, stiff joints and will.
The curls that dared, now have they stared.

On that cottage below, the memories that flow.
Crossing the fields to Mass, feet cushioned by grass.
Between bales of hay, where the cat lay.
Pulls down the blind, for peace of mind.

They were the days, the dew and haze.
Playing on the lawn, dreams of new dawn.

Barking, and half-door, now bones are sore.
Chasing butterflies, the glee, days I still see.

Kieran Reaney

When a person hides their age you know they are insecure. – ***Kieran Reaney.***

By God We Suffered

Black, dark days in Irish history, plagues of
Crooked work, cheating, trickery, gangsterism,
Corruption, oppression, Landlordism, manipulation,
Poverty, famine, evictions, degradation,
Coffin ships, workhouses, Magdalene laundries,
Injustice, bribery, cover-ups, protests, strikes.

Enquiries, Tribunals, bail-outs, betrayal,
Exposés, culprits named and shamed.
Institutions, money missing, squandered,
Not Industrial Schools for girls, strict regimes

In Secondary Schools and National Schools.
Preaching fire and brimstone from frightening
Pulpit, people shaking with psyche-destroying
Fear. Aggression, violence, brutality,
Beaten to a pulp by corporal punishment.

Trust in Holy, religious people,
Priest, Nuns, Bishops left people broken.
Emotional, physical, and sexual abuse, bullying.
Victims frustrated, left with bugger all.
Led astray by people in authority,

Bankers, developers, and so on. Conned by
Lies and fake promises of all governments,
Since the founding of the state.
Jesus suffered for us, we suffered for Him.
God will reward us, we'll have our penance done.

Padraic Reaney

*A snail carries its house on its back, a person carries their cross on their back, and in Ireland, the people at the top screwed up so much, for years and decades, now in this post Celtic Tiger era, the people at the bottom are carrying the country on their backs. – **Padraic Reaney**.*

Lascivious Lassie

He ate the honey and drank the mead.
After other wild dogs, but never did succeed.
He cracked monkey nuts, and spat the shell.
He ate the kernels, but never did swell.

He sat on rails of a table grand.
A cup a tae and pipe in hand.
Like an irritated crocodile, he'd snap very fast.
His loud barking, you would get a blast.

The door-bell ringing, would drive him mad.
Wired by a short fuse, he always had.
Driving sheep over walls, give him a slap.
But if you do that, he'll never come back.

His tail was wagging, lipstick on his collar.
Singing like a busker, give him a dollar.
Put him on a board plane in Shannon.
He'll get his comeuppance, the Grand Canyon.

A year later, the Hollywood Hills, swimming pool.
Sun glasses, neck chain, sips tequila, nobody's fool.
He stretches his paw, she cuddles him hard.
He looks out and winks, "Lassie, you bastard."

Kieran Reaney

*Cowards don't sweat, that's why they are cowards. – **Kieran Reaney**.*

Ye'll Vote For Them Again?

Lazy time, lots of it, all day to do it.
Too many talking shops, not enough
Action shops. "Too many Chiefs, not enough
Indians". Miles too slow making decisions.

Politicians clowning around poli-thick circus.
Going around in circles, like the wheel-of-fortune.
Their numbers always come up.
Side-shows of other issues, like playing

Around with rubbers in offices in the 1980s.
Avoiding the real, hard economic problems.
Wasting valuable time and tax-payers' money.
Kicking political football from post to pillar.

Robbing Peter to pay Paul, point scoring.
They'd have the country back on its feet
In no time, ye didn't believe that, did ye?
Living beyond our means? They certainly are.

Days numbered, loo-sing popularity rapidly.
Clocks ticking in tide, cracking on outside.
Panicking, sinking heavily, septic thinking.
Stinking of corruption, hands tied on that one.

Twine, just like our beloved idyllic island.
Bad management has made a total balls of it.

Padraic Reaney

The straight and narrow is very boring, but outside the straight and narrow is very dangerous. – **Kieran Reaney.**

The great Barbarians team from 1973 who beat New Zealand 23 points to 11 points, in the best rugby match ever played, at the Cardiff Arms Park, on the 27th January 1973. This is the 40th Anniversary. Pictured above are the team, match officials and 3 members of the Barbarians committee. Back row L to R: E. Lewis, G. Windsor-Lewis, **John Pullin (England), W.J. McBride (Ireland), R.M. Wilkinson (England), Derek Quinnell (Wales), Sandy Carmicheal (Scotland), David Duckham (England),** G. Domerceq, D.O. Spyer. Middlerow L to R: **Gareth Edwards (Wales), Mike Gibson (Ireland),** H.L.Glyn-Hughes, **John Dawes (Wales, captain),** H. Waddell, **John Bevan (Wales), Ray McLoughlin (Ireland).** Front row L to R: **Fergus Slattery (Ireland), Tom David (Wales), Phil Bennett (Wales), J.P.R. Williams (Wales).**

Live For The Moment

Time is infinite in both directions, past and future. There is no such thing as the beginning of time because time was always there. Likewise, there is no such thing as the end of time because time is always be there. Even if this world, planet Earth gets destroyed and indeed all its people with it, whenever and for whatever reason or reasons, time will still be there because time can never be wiped out. But what about the present, how does it fit into the time scenario? The present only lasts for a split second in time or a micro-second.

You're probably thinking what's he on about? If you look on your watch now or a clock if you like, and think about five minutes from now, which is the future, and do a count-down of 300 seconds, in a magical flash or like the wink of an eye, on the 300 second mark is the present, and as fast as lightning it goes into the past. It is just like ringing in a New Year, very logical really. There are no time-outs-like in basketball- in real life, because time can never be stopped or frozen.

That split second or micro-second duration of the present can be compared to an imaginary sieve between a person's — male or female — conscious mind and subconscious mind. There is no limit whatsoever regarding how far into the future a person can think about, or indeed imagine with their conscious mind, but when it becomes the present, it goes unbelievably quickly, through the imaginary sieve and into the subconscious mind.

By the same token there is no limit whatsoever in a relationship to how far back into the past a person can think about, or indeed imagine with their conscious mind, but when it becomes the present, it goes through exactly the same don't blink or you'd miss it process, here again through the imaginary sieve and into the subconscious mind. A person can't possibly think or imagine or imagine during the present, for the simple reason that it's over so quickly. As a person is continuing on with their every day living, this process is always in action but they never take any notice of it.

I totally and utterly believe, and am convinced that lots of psychological problems that many people develop, relating to pressure, stress and worry and also the experience of very traumatic events in their lives, or leading very stressful lives, is based on a very simple theory. This theory is that in all these circumstances, the person fails to keep putting all these psychological and emotional — thoughts, feelings, emotions and so on — stuff through the imaginary sieve from the conscious mind to the sub-conscious mind quickly enough.

Consequently the imaginary sieve becomes clogged, blocked up and the person becomes overwhelmed and bogged down, the clock is still ticking away and the person is no longer able to operate in a natural or normal way, and they're wondering what has happened to them, or what has gone wrong. They're totally confused and can't figure it out.

The key to it all is that a person is continuing on with their life, they have to make sure that they are always getting all this psychological and emotional stuff, through this imaginary sieve and into the sub-conscious mind. In other words simply keeping a clear head, but it is obviously easier said than done at times. But if the person does not do this, the trauma, bad experience or whatever will keep cropping up time after time. For example, a person eighty years old may have some issues in their life fifty years prior to that, when they were thirty years old, that they had not dealt with, or put through that magical imaginary sieve and into their subconscious mind.

It is like sweeping a wide factory floor, you have to sweep from wall to wall, and don't leave out any part in between. Whatever age a person may be, and however their life may have gone up to that point, whether it was good, bad or indifferent, if they can accept it with open arms, one hundred per cent, that person has no psychological baggage.

Many people think that the human mind is just inside the head, but it is inside the whole body because it is connected to the nervous system. As a lot of wiring goes through the neck area connecting the brain to the rest of the body, this is why it is so serious if a person breaks their neck, because as this wiring is damaged or severed it leads to the person becoming paralysed from the neck down.

When a person dies their conscious mind goes because they're not conscious, they're dead, and the sub-conscious mind is left, which is the person's soul, and it is released from their body. The soul is a bit like the electrical or electronic black box in an aeroplane. If the aeroplane crashes the black box is used to determine what caused the crash. God determines from the soul what particular person deserves in the hereafter or next life.

What goes into the sub-conscious mind doesn't mean that it never comes up again, of course it can, and often does, but when the person has dealt with it properly, by getting into the sub-conscious mind in the first place, it can do no harm whatsoever, if, and when it comes up again. This is memory, and memory can never be anaesthetized or blotted out fully, but memory does fade with time. As they say, "Time is a Great Healer." When a person is actually experiencing whatever event it is in their life, this is the most powerful time that event is.

Every time that they remember it after that first time, it becomes less and less powerful. They say that a person spends much more time reacting to an event that actually happened to them rather than the event itself. In other words, action once but reaction maybe several times. Of course girls and women are into analysing things big time. Then there is also the interaction between the conscious mind and the sub-conscious mind, or vice-versa, obviously this applies to both men and women.

If a person is very happy and relaxed, at peace with themselves and enjoying themselves, time seems to go very quickly, then on the other side of the coin, if a person is in terrible pain, physically, psychologically or emotionally, time seems to go at a snails pace. The amazing truth is that time always goes at exactly the same pace. Live for the moment, the next moment might be better, and as they say, "Even after the darkest cloud, the sun will always shine."

After all that, I'm now going for a cup of tea and a Time Out, the chocolate bar that is!

Padraic Reaney

Mario Kempes, *guided Argentina to win the World Cup in 1978. Will we see a player of his class in the World Cup in Brazil next year, 2014?*

At Times… There are only 4 basic human emotions, namely happiness, sadness, anger and fear and they are explored in the following 4 poems:

Happiness

Rolling around in laughter.
High as a colourful kite.
Rockin' and reelin' in ecstasy.
Blinded by eternal light.

Padraic Reaney

Sadness

Too low to curse.
Too tired to cry.
Too weary for life.
Don't let my soul die.

Padraic Reaney

Anger

To deliver the killer punch;
In a tough fight.
To put a dagger through his guts,
On a dark night.
To shoot a bullet into his brain,
And not get a fright.
Temper boiling, blood-splattered,
Gory running sight.

Padraic Reaney

Fear

Twisting, turning, nightmare in mind,
Soul jumping, restless in bed.
Pressure, stress, worry of unknown,
High anxiety inside the head.
Panic attack, wet with sweat, gone wild,
Dry throat, feet heavy as lead.
Shaking uncontrollably,
Messages flooding psyché, almost dead.

Padraic Reaney

Voting in an election is like a cat on a cartoon, when he hand a stick to the dog to beat him with. – **Kieran Reaney.**

SARAH Is Good For You

SARAH. Emotionally and psychologically when a person experiences a trauma such as a bereavement for example this is what they go through. But it could also be one of a number of other tough ordeals that many have to face at certain times in their lives. The current recession in this country is causing terrible pain, upset, anxiety and frustration for everyone really and it is breeding negativity and cynicism. In these circumstances people can also experience SARAH.

S is for Shock, A is for Anger, R is for Rejection or in denial that the occurrence ever happened, A is for Acceptance and H is for Healing. These emotions may not always come in that order and more than one can be there at any given time. In fact all five of them could come together sometimes leaving the person feeling very confused. The person might feel so overwhelmed by this emotional maelstrom that they felt they were on auto-pilot, or simply struggling on without any emotion at all. The final piece of the jig-saw is to forgive but this may seem easier said than done at times. As they say," To err is human, to forgive is Divine" and if you don't forgive you'll never heal. The significance of humor as a very powerful therapy tool can never be underestimated, As they say, "Laugh and the world laughs with you, cry and you cry alone".

Padraic Reaney

Truth: *The first person you need to be true to is yourself, if you aren't, you will never be true to anyone else.* – **Padraic Reaney.**

Reality Bites

There was no such thing as the Celtic Tiger, it was all borrowed money. If all the reckless borrowing was paid back by individuals, families, developers and consecutive governments, which has gone on for decades, this country would find itself back in the early 1960s, when massive social change began. Ireland became the second richest country in the world with borrowed money. Hopefully, the borrowers have learned from their mistakes and this country will never see another so-called Celtic Tiger. Borrowed money brought us from the ass and cart to the unreal 'Tiger', and we are now living in the vanquished and dysfunctional country. It will take decades rather than years, if at all, to get out of this recession.

The most honest statement I ever heard from a person in this country was on the Late Late Show on R.T.E. 1 on the 24th of February 2012 when Ryan Tubridy said, "The world is going down the toilet." We have seen a white blackbird in Dublin, two earthquakes in Donegal, one earthquake in Mayo, and a tornado in East Galway recently. The 6 billion people in this world will be very lucky if they don't see Armageddon in the next few years.

But I will finish on a light-hearted note by asking the question. How did a wise Irish, chomping at the bit for a bit, stallion deal with the recession in this country in the 1980s, then the so-called Celtic Tiger and now the current recession? In the 1980s he milked the Social Welfare Cow, then he rode the Celtic Tiger and now he's horseshin' about with a big, broad smile on his face!

Kieran Reaney

Why do people all over the world think the Irish people have a sweet tooth? Because the majority of Irish people, of all ages, are constantly putting their hand in the biscuit tin, to take from a few euro cents to millions of euros. – ***Kieran Reaney.***

Kilcoona Cemetery

In the depths of recession sometimes being negative is positive. – ***Kieran Reaney.***

Eyes Of The Soul

Anthony Raftery, the famous and much appreciated Gaelic poet, lived occasionally in south County Galway and travelled the length and breadth of Ireland, meeting people, discovering various aspects of the country and writing deep and poignant poetry. On these hugely enjoyable excursions he also entertained many people by playing beautiful, sweet music on his fiddle. He was born in Killedan, near Kiltimagh in County Mayo but his date of birth is disputed. In the early part of the 1800s, as part of these enlightening journeys, he visited the parish of Caherlistrane-Kilcoona, and while sheltering from adverse weather conditions near Knockroon, he wrote the poem Seanchas Na Sceiche.

In 1828, what is regarded as the worst boating tragedy ever on Lough Corrib occurred. A number of people departed Annaghdown to travel by boat to attend a fair at Fairhill in Galway City, as there was no road from Annaghdown to Galway at this time. Unfortunately they never reached their destination as the boat sank two miles from Galway, and of the 31 people on board, 20 were drowned. Anthony Raftery recorded and detailed this sad, human disaster in his poem and song Anach Cuain. He died seven years later in 1835 and is buried in Kileeneen Cemetery in Craughwell, County Galway.

As a matter of interest two years later in 1837 The Tuam Herald newspaper was founded and 103 years after the distressing and lamentable catastrophe concerning Annaghdown in 1828, the wearers of the Maroon and White were much happier when they won their first ever County Galway senior football Championship final in 1931. Four years later in 1935, the great playwright Tom Murphy from Tuam was born, a hundred years after the death of Anthony Raftery in 1835. Other well-known North Galway playwrights include M.J. Molly from Milltown and Michael Carey from Headford. Michael Carey and Frank Reaney – uncle of Kieran and Padraic – married two sisters, Michael to Claire Monaghan and Frank to Teresa Monaghan. Michael Carey's brother, Des Carey, was one of Kieran and Padraic's teachers in the National School of Caherlistrane.

In 1895 William Butler Yeats was a guest at Tulira Castle, Labane, and was introduced to Lady Augusta Gregory, from nearby Coole. They become immediate friends and their long and productive association continued for 37 years. W.B. spent many summers in Coole and eventually began living in the old Norman tower house at Thoor Ballylee, within walking distance of Coole. A beautiful local woman named Mary Hynes was celebrated by Anthony Raftery in a delightful poem, decades before this time, in the late 1700s, and W.B. was charmed in reading about this lovely lady, the shining flower of Ballylee. Consequently in Lady Gregory's Kiltartan Poetry Book – published by Cuala Press in 1918 – she translate Raftery's poem from the Irish. "What is the worth of greatness till you have the light of the flower of the branch that is by your side? There is no good to deny it or to try and hide it; she is the sun in the heavens who wounded my heart."

Dr. Douglas Hyde, the first president of Ireland, published Raftery's Poems in 1903. Douglas visited Caherlistrane in the early 1900s and was presented with items of musical heritage by Pat Costello of Feeragh. Pat's daughter was the mother of Rita and Sarah Keane, and Kieran and Padraic's mother, Josephine Costello, was born and reared in the village of Feeragh, and was a first cousin of Rita and Sarah.

Padraic Reaney

To maintain success a person must show more focus and concentration than ever and live one second at a time, but it is also important to balance it with a bit of enjoyment. **– Kieran Reaney.**

Able, Available And Willing

It was late October, Seán and Kate were digging the potatoes with a spade. They were married, Seán was in his early fifties and Kate was forty. They were suddenly interrupted by a twenty-five year old Spailpín who offered to give them a hand 'at the spuds' until the evening. "All right!" said Seán and he continued, "We'll do even better, why don't you stay with us for a few days until they're finished." "I will so," said the spailpín, as he took down his own spade from his shoulder and threw his few belongings on the headland.

That night Seán thought that the spailpín sleeping in a little turf-shed, which was attached to the house and had straw on the floor was too cold, so he suggested the three of them would sleep in the bedroom. It was a small thatched cottage with only a kitchen and one bedroom. Three walls were beside the bed and there wasn't much room for manoeuvre in the rest of the room either.

It was a little bit claustrophobic with the candle quenched but it was cosy. Kate jumped in first beside the wall, then Seán and beside them the spailpín. In the middle of the night Seán heard a noise outside, and he went out to have a look. The goat opened the rope around his neck and had broken into the vegetable patch. Seán had to wait outside for a while to fix the fence. Meanwhile inside, Kate looked at the spailpín and said, "Now's your chance!" When Seán came back the spailpín had returned to his original position, and Seán said, "Brrr, it's a cold wan"

The following evening at the tea, Seán said to the spailpín, "Kate is a fine woman, isn't she?" He continued, "She made that crock of jam from blackberries." "That reminds me," said Kate, "I have to empty the crock of jam under the bed." "You aren't saying much," said Seán to the spailpín. The spailpín smiled, and replied, "I got a crock of gold!" "I didn't see a rainbow," said Seán. The three of them had a good auld laugh.

The spailpín spotted Seán's spade in the corner, which was ready for action, and he said, "I have to go outside to bring in my spade." When the spailpín was gone out, Kate said to Seán, "I'll have to go to see that 'quack doctor' tomorrow to see if he has a lotion or potion for the clap'." "Oh!" said the spailpín, as he stood at the door, "My spade is gone." "Bravo!" said Seán, as he began to clap his hands, "Don't you know you can't trust the bastards around here." The three of them laughed heartily again, and Seán said, "We'll have an early night." The spailpín had a spring in his step as he had loosened the rope on the goat while he was outside.

Kieran Reaney

When a girl is twenty she is always singing, "Just When I Needed You Most." When a woman is sixty she is singing, "Just When I Needed You Moist!" – **Padraic Reaney.**

Connacht Calling

Mid-1990s, hot Summer weather.
"Pale", balmy nights, perspiring buckets.
Disco lights seducing, sexy girl dancing.
Head spinning with alcohol.
Time to make a move.

"Do you come here often?"
He asks confidently.
"The last time I was here,
I can't remember,
Did I come or not," she says.

"You've done the pest,
Now try the best.
Up the West, and to hell
With the rest," he quips.

Padraic Reaney

It's hard enough to get a girl's telephone number during the week, but 'come' Saturday night, if you pardon the pun, after a few drinks or maybe a good few drinks, telephone numbers would be flying, alongside items of the girl's clothing. – **Kieran Reaney.**

Bleeding Spirits

A grave-digger, weather beaten, crocodile skin.
Blistered fingers, prolonged use of shovel and spade.
Crow-bar picking, pick-axe cracking.
Sledge-hammer bursting solid rock.

Mother earth, six foot down, deep thinking.
Blind eyes, veins of corruption, gold diggers.
Shallow burial grounds, card-board euros.
Quick fix blanket of leaves, attacked viciously

By marauding dogs and wild life.
Souls ripped out by brutal Satanism.
A disturbed society not resting in peace.
Jig-saw pieces butchered, cut to shreds.

Irish psyche knifed, forty shades of evil green.
Distressing picture evolving, animal instincts hunting.
Good and righteous dignity savaged by sick atheism.
Going down like an oul' cow, starved of emotion.

Come on, the human being deserves better than this.
Zero vision, remarkable irony.
Lisheens of the past being shown respect.

Padraic Reaney

Some choice: *when a person dies there are some choices. Buried in a graveyard and eaten by worms; cremated, which is against the laws and rules of the Roman Catholic Church, and the cremated person will never go to Heaven and may face eternal damnation; bequeathed to Medical Science, where the body is dissected in a laboratory; buried at sea and eaten by sharks and will there be another one? Buried in the shallow grave in a cardboard box and savage by animals.* - **Kieran Reaney.**

This beautiful garden is at the entrance to our Lady's Holy Well in Kilcoona

Learning Life's Lessons

Talented Senior Club footballer, mid-twenties.
Happy, at peace, enjoying life, delighted
At things going well. Girlfriend walks out on him,
Depths of despair, totally devastated, heart-broken,

Annihilated. Turns to alcohol and drugs for
Comfort, to ease the pain. Overdoses on a cocktail
Of demon drink and cocaine, rushed to the hospital.
Family vigil at bedside, drifting in and out of

Consiousness. Mind and soul entwined,
Roaring, digging deep hole for him. Brain
Short-circuited, gone hay-wire, blow-outs.
Complicated and complex messages, impulses

All over the head-shop. Electrical cables and
Electronic wiring snipped by satan. Stripped
Bare, and re-connected by evil screw-ups.
Control system fried, over-crooked to total

Confusion. Hearing things, seeing weird people,
Climbing onto ceiling, changing to battered
Animals, monstrous fish running from water.
Hallucinating, mermaid girlfriend, swims with

Goldfish. Unplugged sink, ceiling collapsing.
Black panther waiting to pounce. Cycling
On tandem with Goddess, peddling like crazy,
Going to nowhere fast. Dying to get out of this

Hell, helicopter to Heaven. Pulse gets slower,
Dreams slip, sliding. Going slowly through a
Completely white corridor to a new different
Place. He sees the light, God tells him to go

Back. He wakes up, his time wasn't up.
He was one of the lucky ones. He gets,
More time, and a second chance.

Padraic Reaney

People are like animals, they're in bad form most of the time. – **Kieran Reaney.**

President of Ireland Michael D. Higgins and his wife Sabina at a reception in Áras an Uachtarain celebrating the victory by St. Brendan's National School, Kilmeena, Newport, Co. Mayo in the inaugural Get Involve Community Initiative competition. Photograph courtesy Local Newspaper Week 2013.

Cream Always Comes To The Top

Eamon De Valera, romantic visions for Éireann,
Eamon O'Cuiv, senior, Politician,
Eamon O'Cuiv, junior, footballer,
Clonbur's glory, All-Ireland Champions.
Y-people definitely have the X-factor.

Henry and Enda Kenny, Mayo magic,
Cora from Carnacon, "Simply The Best",
Here's to you Mrs. Robinson,
Croagh Patrick and Knock Shrine,
Footsteps to a brighter future, Croke Park?

Dr. Douglas Hyde, Early soldier,
Dermot from Ros', a true leader,
William Butler, sleeping eternally,
Ben Bulben, Yeats County.
"Go West, young man", West Life.

John McGahern, amongst lovely women,
The West is calling, great pedigree,
Overflowing talents and abundant skills,
Steer clear of the iceberg.
Michael D. Higgins, inspirational poet,

Saffron and Blue Captain of Irish ship,

Slowly, gently, surely, guiding us back,
To the Island we loved so well.
"An ounce of breeding is better
Than a tonne of feeding".

Padraic Reaney

Some people are prepared to lose money to suppress talent. – **Kieran Reaney.**

At 22 years of age, Prince Alfred gained a throne and saved a Kingdom. David Hemmings, in the lead role, as Alfred, (above) in a still from the 1968 film Alfred the Great. A substantial part of the film was shot on Knockma Hill. Above photograph courtesy of Metro Goldwyn Mayer.

Memories Of Alfred The Great

From March until November '68.
Tinseltown was beside our gate.
Array of stars, permanent flair.
Hollywood and Metro Goldwyn Mayer.

Knockma Hill and the glamour.
Swords, shields and the clamour.
Michael York and the Danes.
Saxon David Hemmings that reigns.

Ian McKellen now called Sir.
Memories and nostalgia now stir.

Jocelyn Rickards had the honour.
Of marrying director Clive Donner.

Sinéad Cusack and Prunella Ransome.
Charming, ravishing and handsome.
The Belclare Sports that Day.
Wanting them, to forever stay.

Kieran Reaney

The person that is very tough and strong mentally does their own thinking. They can't be brainwashed by anyone or anything. – **Padraic Reaney.**

No Strings Attached

Ireland in the past, 'bad' girls locked up in Magdalen laundries, so-called 'good' girls holding out watching marriage. Paddy caught between a rock and a 'hard' place, drinking pints of porter, falling between two stools, trying to find ways of releasing his wild animal urges. Eureka, he found a solution, street-wise barman tells him to 'take a boat', go across the pond'. "There's nothing in Éire only bad weather, man, say goodbye to Bob your uncle before you go, and when you arrive on the other side, say hello to aunt Fanny!" He took the barman's advice and so Paddy's sex life started in Hollyhead.

Fast forward to later times, feminist movement 'takes off', mná na hÉireann pushing for fair rights, equality, human rights, girl power, we're just as good as men, even better at some things, no longer want to be mens' slaves, women doing their own thinking, fair play to ye ladies, men saluted ye.

Fast forward again, contraception became widely available; but the amazing irony is that there are more unwanted pregnancies now than ever. Men and women began cohabitating – which destroyed marriage (heterosexual marriage obviously) and the family unit – years ago if a man wanted a woman he had to put a ring on her finger first, at the present time if a man wants a woman all he has to do is give her a ring on her door bell.

Divorce eventually was introduced, now they're pushing for abortion, homosexual marriage, lesbian marriage, gay people allowed to rear children. Other issues they're wondering about in recent times are women priest, euthanasia, assisted suicide, allowing prenuptial agreements for farmers wishing to get married – afraid they'll lose their few acres if she does a runner – nuclear power and atheism in schools.

As the songs says, "It is a world crazy or peculiar, ladies are dancing alone, frontmen all want to be backmen, and the backmen all want to go home". Where is it all going to end?

Padraic Reaney

In 1990 a saying Irish people heard a lot was, "Timofte versus Bonner." At the present time in this country, nearly all young lads have a saying on the tip of their tongue in relation to girls which is: "Get 'em off there faster." – **Kieran Reaney.**

It's The Way It Has Gone

Astonishing, astounding, breathtaking, beautiful girls, goddesses from Venus, dressed to thrill, as a young as late teens, sex kittens, sex bombs ready to explode, acting and behaving macho, go out at weekends, nights on the town, some of them have more f- words said in half an hour than many football team managers would say in a year.

High heels, not healed, legs that seem to be never ending, stairways to Heaven, grey-hound minis, not far away from the 'hare'. G-strings that would fit in a match-box, boobs scarcely covered by bras defying the law of gravity, to let, up for grabs. Heavily made up, and wearing expensive jewellery.

Cigarettes, drink, drugs optional to make the night more enjoyable. Knowing so much about the 'wild thing' they could easily write their own version of the Karma Sutra. Their grannies never saw a man naked until their honeymoon night, and their grandfathers just know where Percy went.

You can go the full monty now, Paddy, just as easy as our forefathers enjoyed a kiss and a cuddle, naturally, no problem, no strings attached. This is our new modern country, Paddy never had it so good, some of these girls are naturals at it, you would have to get up for the rest, and the best of it all is that you can get it at home now, Paddy.

Padraic Reaney

The only difference between an ordinary girl screwing around and a 'pro' is the money. – **Kieran Reaney.**

The boat, Isle Of Innisfree, on Lough Corrib, beside Ashford Castle, in Cong. County Mayo. 'I will arise and go now and go to Innisfree, and a small cabin built there, of clay and wattles made." W.B. Yeats.

Costly Mistakes Are Breeding Cynicism

All Irish Governments, since the very beginning, failed miserably, the political system never worked, too much emphasis on 'Mé Féin', neglected to pay back debts, to balance the books properly. "Let the next 'shower' worry about it", attitude, "Who cares? As long as we get through it ourselves." Eventually it all catches up on them, as we all know too well, like a mischievous cat that ravelled the ball of wool in an old lady's knitting basket, or the proverbial bad chef that made a balls of the cabbage.

Joining the Euro led to 'rip-off' Ireland, prices rounded up. NAMA, 'No Answers More Ale'. The now septic banks horsed out money, like it was going out of fashion, seemingly without collateral or security. They became so greedy that they risked it all by getting into gambling with money, and they lost the shirts on their backs. Now they're paying the fool's price, white coloured pencil policy of Judges, make a laughing stock out of them in the Courts. "Sure he can pay back a few euros a week, he'll have his debt cleared in a few hundred years time, they can wait for their money."

The bank workers are left playing around with figures as they try desperately hard to 'figure' this one out, with an odd grey hair beginning to appear, you can bet your bottom dollar, as the top bucks get their asses kicked. Developers and builders got obsessed by bricks and mortar, farmers were also into this way of thinking, but who could blame them, as the banks were shovellin' out the dosh'.

But it's much easier to turn cash into concrete than concrete into cash. But they all totally missed the point, which was that, firstly, the population of the country was miles too small to want all these houses, apartments, office blocks, and so on, and secondly, most of the people simply hadn't got the money, an outrageous miscalculation for all concerned. Not paying heed to a basic or fundamental law of business, as regards whatever service is being provided, " Is there a market for it?"

This is common sense, not rocket science, lads. Apart from the 'big three' already mentioned, the government, the Banks and the Developers, lots of other professional people, or individuals at the 'top' were pushing the rules to say the least, with people in certain situations, and these unfortunate people were the victims of raw deals that they never deserved.

Padraic Reaney

In any and every aspect of life the person that does not go into it with realistic expectations will end up very disappointed and totally disillusioned. – **Padraic Reaney.**

Gospel Truth

In Ireland or indeed any country in the world how the whole system works, or how it often doesn't work, is very simply based on two-tier set-up, namely the people at the top and the people at the bottom. Many individuals in this country are constantly pointing their fingers at the people at the top, as regards the outrageous collapse of the total economy and indeed all system all across the board, and this is very accurate and justified.

But apart from the Government, he Bankers, the Developers and lots of other so-called professional people at the top, many people at the bottom were by no means Saints or Angels either, by getting all types of different mortgages from Banks, loans from Credit Unions and all the rest of it. They were living beyond their means – now where did I hear that before – in other words they wanted every luxury and comfort, but they hadn't the money to pay for it, and it seems at this point in time, a lot of this money is never going to be paid back.

Or maybe in a hundred, or two hundred, or three hundred years time, according to newspaper reports of court proceedings, in money to be paid back that is owed cases. The people at the top trying to screw the people at the bottom and vice-versa. This is part of the classic game of life. Come on, play the game!

Padraic Reaney

A stoic person has too much respect for his life and thinks modesty is part of honesty. -**Kieran Reaney.**

Greatest Let Down Of All

Last by no means least, in fact the worst wine of the lot, was the straw that broke the camel's back, and put the final nail in the coffin of annihilation of this country. Yes! You've guessed it, Religion, the Roman Catholic Church. Huge numbers of people were heavily, totally and utterly committed to God, spiritually, Christianity, complete trust in Priest and Nuns and the niceness, goodness and righteousness that they thought was part of it.

They believed it without the shadow of doubt, and were thoroughly convinced that the slightest bit of controversy associated with it, would never happen, not in a million years. This whole, heart and soul area of Irish life, was vitally important to many of the people, and it was so serious that it has seen as a matter of life or death, giving their lives leadership, direction and meaning.

In fact their big time religious beliefs and convictions, were instrumental in getting them out on their beds in the morning. They had something to live for, which was ultimately to live their lives for God, and indeed to die for God when their time is up, and He called them home. They realized and knew that as regards this life, they were only passing through.

As bad and all as it was, for all the other systems, in their beloved Emerald Isle to go dreadfully under, all across the board, due to greedy avarice and sick, satanist corruption, they never thought, not even for a split second of time, in their most outrageous nightmares, that the Hierarchy would let them down also, and brutally betray them.

After all, these holy people were supposed to lead by example, but a certain group of them were preaching one thing and practising another. They blew it sky high, screwed it up, puns definitely intended, and knocked what had been built up for years and decades. They drained the real nature out of the Irish people, and busted and destroyed their psyche. The island of Saints and Scholars began to die a very sad, lonely and painful death.

The happy, peaceful rug had been pulled aggressively from beneath them, and now they are left to wander in the wilderness like headless chickens. The preposterous rise and fall of the so-called Celtic Tiger era has resulted in a huge sense of loss, confusion, uncertainty, lack of spirit and hopelessness in its wake.

Padraic Reaney

If you stand up to bullying, corruption, badness or evil it crumbles very quickly because it's built on quicksand. Righteousness and goodness are built on solid rock and can never be brought down. – **Padraic Reaney.**

Pitiful Politics

Approximately six months after this present recession kicked in seriously, I received a letter in the post from a well-known Politician. In it he stated that they were looking for ideas regarding getting things done, that would assist in keeping the economic mess at bay, because they knew, even at that early stage, that the disaster was gathering momentum rapidly and everything was going downhill fast. He also gave information about an open meeting that was penciled in to go ahead about two weeks later.

The following day I had a telephone conversation with him that lasted around half-an-hour. My plan was in connection with the unfinished, ghost housing estates. Basically it was about getting the lads and girls doing Apprenticeship courses, in all the building and construction Trades, in all the FÁS training centres, go to those ghost estates with their respective Instructors, and gain very valuable on-the-job work experience, by completing the projects. Then eventually the fully built houses could be sold off at cheap rates to people in dire need of accommodation. This is not rocket science, it is common sense, National School stuff.

He said that he thought it was a great idea, and would definitely bring it up at the meeting and contact me again to discuss it further. I don't honestly know did the meeting ever take place because that was the last I heard about it. Obviously the idea wasn't taken on board anyway because the appalling situation is the same on this issue a few years later.

As they say, time is money, and the longer the time meter stays running the more shillings the Politicians get out of it. At this stage, with glass broken maliciously on doors and windows, copper piping and cylinders stolen and widespread vandalism on some of these housing areas, a lot of it is gone down the tubes. Recently it was stated in the media that the Government are now proposing to have some of these ghost estates demolished.

What a waste, but then when did Politicians ever care about the people? As the Politicians keep screwing things up the tax-payers keep footing the bill. Anyone that still believes in Irish Politics are quite frankly worse than the Politicians, and deserve the raw deals that they're getting. Unfortunately some people never learn.

Padraic Reaney

The hallmark of a great leader is simply having the right attitude.
If they have, the sky is the limit. If they haven't, they are beaten
before a ball is kicked in it. – ***Padraic Reaney.***

Sizzling Similarities

Coinciding with the Celtic Tiger era in Ireland there was a relatively small Sexual Revolution but many people didn't seem to be aware of it. In a strange way it resembled the swinging sixties in England but obviously on a much smaller scale. Across the pond, whether John Profumo affair in 1963 – when two call girls, Christine Keeler and Mandy Rice-Davies brought down the English Government- triggered it all off is debatable, but it certainly added fuel to it.

Eventually even the people got over the outrageous shock of it all, and it was sorted out, more or less, the attitude to sex and sexuality became much more relaxed, taken in its stride. This year 2013 is the 50th Anniversary of that event and a book has been written recalling the whole story. Also the brilliant film Scandal, from 1989, gives the viewer a remarkable insight into all the activity.

It was the most controversial film of that year, starring Joanne Whalley as Christine Keeler, Bridget Fonda as Mandy Rice-Davies, John Hurt, Sir Ian McKellen of Alfred the Great fame, Britt Ekland, and lead singer with the Fine Young Cannibals, Roland Gift, who plays a cameo role towards the end of the film.

In one famous scene in one of the Club's, where there were several members of the English government and other people of high power, the girls were dressed up as Indians, with the 1953 hit song by Guy Mitchell, She Wears Red Feathers playing at the background.

The chorus went like this: "She wears red feathers and a hooly-hooly skirt. She lives on just cokey-nuts and fish from the sea. A rose in her hair, a gleam in her eyes and love in her heart for me." The film Scandal made over 8 million dollars profit at the Box Office.

Four decades prior to this there was a comparable occurrence in America, in the roaring twenties, when greed, big spending, extravagance, hedonism and sexual promiscuity were the order of the day – or night – and very much on tap. As they say all good – or bad, depending on which way you want to look at it – things must come to an end, and so it did here, because it all ended with the Wall Street Crash in 1929.

This period of history has been recorded in a book, and also in films, about a flamboyant fictitious character from that time, named Jay Gatsby, and they're titled The Great Gatsby. Consequently the following years in America, were of the leaner variety, not as much meat on the oul' bone if you know what I mean! After a storm there comes a calm and this was also experienced by our neighbours across the water, in the aftermath of the 1960s, as things seemed to drop and become more placid!

With the strict austerity measure to continue in Ireland, not alone for years but decades, in this post Celtic Tiger trauma, many people in this country now realise that they were playing a fool's game, or as the song says, "It started out in Heaven, it ended up in tears."

Co-written by Padraic and Kieran Reaney

When a lap dancing girls get pregnant, her friends say, "She's up the pole." As regards posters, when there is an election, all politicians' helpers are up the pole.

– Padraic Reaney.

Bird's Eye View. *A sea gull, perched on top of a street light, watches anxiously on other birds' below as they search for food in Galway Shopping Centre.*

At the top, ironically, there is a lot more isolation than adulation. **– Kieran Reaney.**

City Bird

In Galway City.
Standing so pretty.
Her radiant smile.
She's so docile.

Her red hair.
Compelled to stare.
Mesmerized by charm.
Heart so warm.

An ageing dream.
A train's steam.
Even on snow.
She will glow.

Like sea gulls fly.
Towards the sky.
Meals and snacks.
And carrier packs.

Kieran Reaney

Don't get upset by the fact that life is only a game. – ***Padraic Reaney.***

Stains Of Sin

"Don't put temptation in their way girls, men have no self-control, they are driven and ruled by their primitive urges, animal instincts. Liathroidín full, brain empty, take care, beware."

Girls night out, lots of drink, soft foolish talk, don't pay heed to those penguins, what would they know about it, not as if they're talking from experience, the next one they see will be their first. Babes rolling around with laughter, if you can't be good be careful, if you can't be careful, buy a pram.

Boy meets girl, going out together for a while. Babies cause accidents in cars, accidents in cars cause babies. Fast and abstain, if you must do it, don't take pleasure on it. He says, "If you loved me you would." She says, 'If you loved me you wouldn't.' He says, "If you don't, I'm out of here."

Catch 22 situation, pressure, bullying, manipulation, she loves him, she doesn't want to lose him, she agrees, to please him. He has his wicked way with her, it's all so fast, over very quickly, no time for any stain, they should have walked, not raced, they should have made love and not haste.

No precautions taken, girl gets pregnant, still a teenager, decent respectable family, shamed, embarrassed, can't handle it, father flips, she has to put away. Behind the high, solid , fethered walls of a Maggie's Nest, to be humiliated, intimidated, degraded, scrubbing her fingers to the bone, cleansing her soul, as she washes away the stains of sin.

Padraic Reaney

Irish girl falls in love, Irish man falls on top of her. – ***Padraic Reaney.***

Galway…Races

Fast people, fast horses,
Fast girls, fast jockeys,
Fast cars, fast food,
Fast drink, fast money,
Fast city, fast living,
Fast thinking, slow roundabouts!

Padraic Reaney

If a doer was more of a thinker he wouldn't have to do next or near as much. – **Padraic Reaney.**

Horses relaxing in Kilcoona.

In this country, with bad weather and the recession, and lack of spirit in the country, when a man turns fifty, he discovers a new pleasure in life, sleep. – **Kieran Reaney.**

Horses For Courses

Champagne, chair-o-planes, chilblains,
Lager, swagger, stagger.
Big shots, low shots, small shots,
Shots of whiskey, shots-a-penny.
Hobbyhorses, swinging boats, knick-knacks,
Wheel-of-fortune, roulette.
Paddy Joe, Michael Joe, Tommy Joe,
Martin Joe, Jolly Joe.

Stallions, flutes, tea-chests, big chest,
Hairy chests, miniskirts.
Riflemen, physios, psychos, weirdos,
Winos, homos, hobos.
Mares, flares, voyeurs, exhibitionists,
Studs, geldings, whores.
Straights, queers, quares,
Lesbos, bisexuals, transexuals.

Horseboxes, fish, chips, chicks,
Ice cream, tote double, double brandy.
Shades, suedes, helicopters, all-night rockers,
Yobs, balloons with knobs.
Brollies, umbrellas, sombreros, stilettoes,
Herds, nerds, geeks, Jeeps.
Drunks, hunks, monks, punks,
Pastries, cupcakes, buns, sconed, stoned.

Tattoos, cute hoors, bicycles,
Tricycles, tripods, try sexuals.
Frothy pints, frolics, high heels,
Well-heeled respectables, bespectacled.
Hashish, cocaine, heroin, funkies,
Junkies, broom, magic mushroom.
Cowboys, charmers, jeans torn, porn,
Horn, forlorn, riffraff, tours, beuers.

Hawkers, punters, Hillman Hunters,
Wibbly wobbly wonders, hikers, bikers.
Bandanas, piercings, fleecings, janitors,
Gamblers, chancers, bankers, wankers.
Day dreamers, go-betweeners, inbetweeners,
Three card trick, bluff, snuff.
Buff, muff, auld guff, puffing cigarettes,
Great stuff, wuff-wuff.
Bookies outspoken, apple tarts, girl stunner,
"Get 'em off," Fred Hoff, fuck off.

Kieran Reaney

A man that is getting old cannot go back to Woodstock. – **Kieran Reaney.**

Losing It In Galway City

Centenary year of the G.A.A.,
Quincentenary of Galway City, 1984,
A city – and indeed country-
Steeped in history, heritage, culture,
People, stories and memories.

Che Guevara to be honoured,
By Maroon and White?
"Forever Young", famous fountain,
Eternally overflowing,
With unrivalled beauty,
Magnetic urban masterpiece.

Fourteen Stations of the Cross,
Fourteen Tribes of Galway,
Athy, Blake, Bodkin, Browne,
Darcy, Deane, Ffont, Ffrench,
Joyce, Kirwan, Lynch, Martin,
Morris, Skerrett,
What would they think
About this issue?

So many brilliant Galwegians,
Male and female, past and present,
Much too numerous to mention,
Would truly, genuinely and sincerely,
Deserve to be honoured first.

How would it effect the
Irish-American relationship?
Beautiful Éire, going down,
Deeper into desperate, depressing,
Spiritless, zero inspirational,
No glimmer of light,
At the end of a very dark tunnel,
No speck of hope recession.

Euros are as scarce as hen's teeth,
We can't afford to get on
The wrong side of the Yanks.
"Build a ladder to the sky,
And climb on every rung",

But make sure that you're
Climbing the right ladder.
Get real, grow up, for God's sake.

Padraic Reaney

*Flattery is a way of manipulation. It is often used by politicians to get people to support them. – **Padraic Reaney.***

The altar inside the entrance to Our Lady's Holy Well in Kilcoona.

Table Quiz

Lovely Helen of Troy.
Do you ever lie?
The Green and Red.
Now in good stead.

Young Niamh Cinn Óir.
"Knockin' On Heaven's Door."
A rock star steams.
As the guitar dreams.

A beer so light.
But what a fright.
No-one will flee.

From 'the bumble bee'.

Deirdre, cool and quiet.
By the candlelight.
Another night, the prize.
We'll reach the skies.

Kieran Reaney

By degrees: *Writing a book is like hitting a massive rock with a sledgehammer, for days or weeks or months, but eventually after an awful lot of hard work, you get over the 'gain line' in rugby terms, you feel you have 'cracked it' and you begin to see the finished product at the end of the tunnel. –* ***Kieran Reaney.***

Out Of It

Immature guy, late teens, no experience of life.
Foolish, innocent to the harsh reality of naivety.
Stumbles out from Night-club, dazed, sleepy.
Tranquillisers taken earlier, washed down by,

Whiskey and brandy, drowning his lonely sorrows.
Unsteady on his feet, balance deteriorating rapidly.
Drowsily he enters take-away and orders,
"A bag of chicken and a breast of chips, a litre of

Beer and twenty cigars," in a slurred tone of speech.
A tough gent at the end of the queue says,
"Get out, you'd burst the breathalyser, ya hure ya."
He hurriedly rushes out, getting tripped at the door.

Managing to stay upright he struggles to the car-park.
Eventually he finds his car and wearily rests his body.
His head is thumping. "Help me make it through
The night." He attempts to get the car keys

Into the ignition, but he can't do it.
The blazing fire of his whole being is quenched.
He's drained, drenched, his soul turns to ashes.
He collapses on top of the steering wheel.

Padraic Reaney

Facing reality: *In this life there are three things that most human beings would wish for or want: to live forever, to remain young forever, and to be high, happy and at peace all the time. Unfortunately any one or all of these three things has never happened nor never will happen in this life, but in Heaven you could get all three.* – **Padraic Reaney.**

Reincarnation

High-heeled claws, cute paws.
Lovely fur, gentle purr.
Miniskirt, stocking flirt.
Red roses, metempsychosis.

Ramblin' fields, paltry deals.
Whiskers guide, excited inside.
Wild night, morning light.
Heart breaks, snowflakes.

Tears flow, so low.
No furl, same girl.

Kieran Reaney

Life is limited: *In all aspects of life there are limits: an athlete, male or female, will never clear twenty feet in the high jump, or jump fifty feet in the long jump.* – **Padraic Reaney.**

Porter-Head-Work

A drunken, confused, loquacious, older Irishman making love with his wife. He is in the mood for talking and maybe letting off a bit of steam. "Some men become very successful by using their big heads. A lot of men screw up their lives by doing miles too much thinking with their small heads. Many a big sporting occasion was lost by a quick rush of blood to the head, not keeping a cool head.

For the majority of men the small head rules the big head. The small head seems to have a mind on its own. It's the lightest thing in the world, sure his imagination can lift it. Not so sure about that when he gets older though. A few pints swallowed, brewer's droop and all that. What's home without a mother? What's a pint without another?

One swallow never made a Summer, or a jar never made a man lustful, "where's Rover? Me oul' dog, me oul' flower, me best friend, no good at card-playing though, sure he wags his tail every time he gets a good hand, or paw should I say. He wanders into a hair-dressing salon in n intoxicated state looking for the man that shot his Pa. I ramble in after him looking for a wash, cut and a blow-job. Take everything but blows you crazy fool. Old Mother Hubbard went to the cupboard to get her dog Rover a bone, but as she bent over, rover took over, and showed her a bone of his own. He couldn't keep it in his trouser, the dirty dick.

Is there a party down in Fanny's house. I'm after seeing Dick goin' in the front door. The front door, the back door, the side door, the hall door, the trap door, those bucks are game for anythin' man. You'd want to be careful of the trap door though, because you couldn't be left with a leaking boat and paddle. You might be as well off paddling your own canoe. Sure most of the time these married birds don't want to hear about it. The birds with the feathers are the soundest of the whole feicin' lot.

Two heads are better than one they say, a lot harder to keep two heads quite though. Ticking over nicely, like an old Ford I'm slow to start but when I get going – into the rhythm of things like – it's not easy to stop me. Earth girls are easy, Ha! Ha! Never knew any alien girls, or are they all alien? After a few years of marriage, a couple start doing it doggy style, the husbands stands up and begs, and the wife turns over and plays dead!

Many women get on in life, and make mighty money out of giving good head, take your time there woman, you have a head-start on me. Take your time, don't start without me, hold on, I'm getting into the swing of things, hold on. Holding on for a hero, hero days how are ya?

We're flyin' it now, Peggy, the monster with the three heads, where's your leggy?" "Down there." "Down where?" "Where, Tammy?" "Where, Tammy?" A slip of the tongue. "How's she cuttin'?" "What's wrong with ya?" "I'm parched with the thirst." "You're all talk and no action, shut your mouth you foolish twat!" she says.

She continues, "You're driving me nuts, like a cranky shagin' squirrel that has lost his nuts." He then says with a full load of energy, "I'm comin' like a "Bat Out

Of Hell." She then says angrily, "You're as blind as a bug in a badger's backside, sure you aren't in at all yet you stupid ass-hole!"

Padraic Reaney

As regards girls, fun and games with them and eroticism, the far majority of men never grow up. – **Padraic Reaney.**

Only Messin'

Bankers mess around with your money.
Doctors mess around with your body.
Psychiatrists mess around with your head.
Females mess around with your emotions.

Priest and Nuns mess around with your soul.
Injustice and unfairness mess around
With your heart.
Temptation and boredom mess around
With your sexuality.

Politicians mess around with your sanity.
The weak person allows this to happen.
The strong person doesn't, peace man, don't panic,
Enjoy yourself, life is beautiful.

Padraic Reaney

At time it's important to call a spade a spade, but if a person isn't generally positive, they will not achieve, and they will be unable to look forward to events effectively, and they will not ne able to enjoy themselves fully either. – **Kieran Reaney.**

Pole Dance

Writhing, sensual dance.
Take a chance.
In the mood.
You're no prude.

In my hand.
Soft and grand.

Flicked at me.
All the glee.

Like a snake.
A serpent awake.
Meander and twist.
Bright light mist.

Moon drips fear.
Sweat crystal clear.
The body glows.
The passion flows.

Like all men.
Let them spin.
Red apple ate.
Briefs white bait.

Bare souls old.
But never cold.
Beliefs will lie.
Then they'll die.

Kieran Reaney

There's nothing for nothing: In a circus very skillful and talented poodles, are rewarded with sweet niceties by their beautiful lady boss, for performing a great trick. In life a hard working and dedicated husband, is rewarded after his week of tough graft, by his wife boss on a Saturday night, by allowing him to have his wicked way with her. – **Padraic Reaney.**

Natural and built heritage near Kilcoona Graveyard.

Hard-Up Oul' Lads

Strict Roman Catholic up-bringing in the family home. Religious beliefs a huge part of every-day living. Teachers in National School promote this integral portion of Irish life. January 1st 1973, locking horns with Europe, E.E.C. prices and Paddy wage, a new era dawns, shooting from the hip, into the abyss, no-where, communal community camouflage.

High Mass, giants of Priest, boxers, bouncers, big in stature, small in character, togging-in, talking about and looking forward to big meal in Hotel after funeral, after some-one is put down into the cold clay. Remember you're just a number man. Unbelievable hypocrisy – Ireland was always famous for that – mixed messages. Signed : Confused.

Rewind to one hour earlier. All through Mass, back seats of church, who cares whether it's men's side or women's side, oul' lads continue to read hot newspapers, reading between the legs, ogling scantily clad girls, drooling unashamedly, sexcited, heads – both heads – filled with red raw lust, smiling with satisfaction, elbowing, pinching each other, making sure the other lad saw what Doctors see, through the key-hole voyeurism, fine tits of stuff, ye'd give them 'a good wan'. No respect from horny hures.

Qutside the Church, a biteen of pressure showing on an inside leg of the trousers. On the way home in a Hillman Hunter, are a childless, frustrated couple. A cynical neighbor once said about them. "Why wouldn't they be childless, when she never let him take it out of the wrapper." The prude wife says to her husband, "What's wrong with ya, you're doing quare driving, be careful or you'll gup on the wall." He says nothing but thinks to himself, "I'm feeling so randy now, I'd gup on a cracked plate."

After arriving home the wife is stressed out, in the kitchen in a broth of perspiration – and no inspiration – cooking the curlew for the dinner, hoping that it doesn't burn. She thinks to herself, "I'm suffering from 'the burn' me-self, and it has nothing whatsoever to do with a place in the bathroom, burning with passion, sweating furiously, and cooking his own chicken. Is he from the Farmer relief service? Up she flew!

Padraic Reaney

In life a wise man always starts with the end in mind. – **Padraic Reaney.**

Christy Brown (1932-1981) was born in Dublin and suffered from cerebral palsy causing paralysis in his arms and legs. He won his first painting competition at the age of 12 and he is well known for the film based on his famous book My Left Foot which was made in 1989 and directed by Jim Sheridan. It starred Daniel Day Lewis who won an Academy award for Best Actor. A year later in 1990, the film The Field was made in Aasleigh and Leenane in Connemara. Adapted from John B. Keane's 1965 play, and also directed by Jim Sheridan, it starred Richard Harris, John Hurt, Tom Berenger, Seán Bean and Jenny Conroy, who has relatives near Tuam. Part of the film was shot near Gaynor's pub in Leenane, which is where our aunt Vera's husband, Mickey Gaynor, came from. In 1996, An Post, the Irish Post Office issued a set of postage stamps to commemorate the Centenary of Irish Cinema, 1896 to 1996.

Photo courtesy of MFPA, Pineview, Firhouse Road, Dublin 16.

Girl Power

During the Celtic Tiger years in Ireland girl power was in vogue big time and going from strength to strength, with brave and courageous women coming forward to stand up and be counted for Mná na h-Éireann. The two Mary's took the top honours during that era, with Mary Robinson making history by becoming the first woman President of Ireland in 1990, for her seven year term until 1997. Mary McAleese followed eagerly and enthusiastically these huge steps for woman-kind by becoming the second woman President of the Green, White and Gold, by fulfilling a fourteen year double term from 1997 to 2011. Consequently a unique chapter in Irish history was written.

Padraic Reaney

Successful people have to be able to close doors on some other people because some other people will as sure as hell close doors on them. – **Kieran Reaney.**

Making Cents Of It All

For years and indeed decades after the famine in Ireland, 1844 to 1849, - regarded by many people worldwide as the worst human tragedy of the Nineteenth Century – great writers such as Tom Murphy from Tuam, and Walter Macken were producing brilliant literary works on this time theme. In the Twentieth Century there were two outrageously disastrous events, namely the two world wars, the First World War, 1914 to 1919, and the Second World War, 1939 to 1945. Amazingly both of these World Wars occurred during the first half of that Century, with only twenty years between the end of the first one, and the beginning of the second one.

If and when there is a Third World War, more than likely it would go nuclear, and the human race will be wiped out very quickly. God will never end the world because he loves it and its people too much, even with all the evil of many people, He still loves them because God's love is infinite. How long the human race continues is entirely and totally in man's and indeed woman's own hands. It is a person's mind that controls their hands. This is free will, one of God's great gifts to people.

However, back to the past. In my opinion, for years to come, many people will be creating their own take, in any and every form of the Arts really on how Ireland went from boom to bust, in the rise and ultimately devastating fall of the so-called Celtic Tiger era, generally and broadly speaking, and for the sake of round figures, 1990 to 2010. The euphoric high and shattering low of a nation, gone lunatic mad with insanely easy, gone lunatic mad with the insanely easy availability of euros, no euro vision here banking bucks.

Apart from the total collapse of Irish economy, which was a dagger through the psyche of its people, the brutally painful overall consequences were much deeper, as this was only part of the full picture. To be perfectly honest, every system in the country failed miserably, all across the land, and in this prolonged funeral, the once proud Green, White and Gold flag is tattered and torn, battered and bruised, and flying very low with broken wings.

As the wheels of the clocks of time, slowly and surely turn, as the countdown to 2016 continues, people remember the seven brave and courageous men, who unselfishly gave their lives for Ireland. Ironically in its recent history, people at the top gave their country for their lives. Many Irish people would have thought years ago, as the Centenary of 1916 would be drawing closer, that there would be a thirty-two county united Ireland, everyone very happy, at peace with each other and pulling together, but the alarming, sad reality is that it could not be much further away from that, the way it is at the present time.

They say that a person lives their life forward, and try to make sense out of it looking back. While huge numbers of Irish people are getting taken to the cleaners footing the bill, and wrecking their brains trying to figure it out, wondering how and where it all went wrong, and indeed where all the money went, as they walk wearily to the soup kitchens, or perhaps to Pieta House, the politicians continue to make their own cents out of it, millions of euros in fact. While the Irish Government continue to screw things up in luxury, the Irish people struggle on in misery.

Padraic Reaney

The people at the top, driven by power and avarice, are always grabbing too much of the cake. Sometimes, if a person is too greedy, they could lose everything. The less a person has the more they see. – **Padraic Reaney.**

All The Same

"I'll bring the horse to the blacksmith to get new horseshoes," said the peasant to his son. "All right," said his son. 'I'll be working with the sickle until you get back." The peasant tells the blacksmith that the landlord is overcharging him for rent on the house, and says, "I'll murder that landlord, one of these days." The blacksmith, as he is hammering the horseshoes on the anvil, begins to get a little bit afraid and starts to worry. No more is spoken between them until the job is finished. The blacksmith tells the peasant that the cost of the job is okay for a month or two, which makes the peasant very grateful, and he thanks the blacksmith.

Twelve year-old Charlotte says, "Excuse me, Momah, I hope I'm not disturbing you, as you are so totally absorbed in you complex crochet pattern.' She then gently leaves her intriguing novel on the solid oak table, and says, "Our old dog Belvedere is near the front door and looking back worriedly. I'll let him out, Momah, so that he can go to the back garden and empty his aching bladder behind the big sycamore tree. Okay, Momah, I hope that doesn't disturbed Papah, who is heavily concentrating on his study of complicated calligraphy. I'll put another block of wood into the blazing open fire now, Momah, and I have to say the gamekeeper is a pleasant chap. I saw him come into the kitchen yesterday with some rabbits and wild fowl, to give to the maid, so that she could prepare the food." "Perhaps you better avoid that young man, dear," said her father, "which reminds me, I'll be taking out one of the horses after dinner to join the hunt."

Twelve year-old Petrina – who is very grown up for her age – is involved in a serious argument with her attractive mother, who is furiously smoking a cigarette, as she desperately tries to stay calm. Petrina wants permission to go to school Disco, before she starts secondary school. Her father, in a white singlet, is thrown up in the couch, flicking through the satellite television channels, looking for something 'hot' to watch, and drinking cans of beer. With the corner of his eye he notices the dog near the front door and says, "Fuck ye, what are ye at? Our old dog Beldevere wants to go out the hure, he's dyin' for a good oul' slash."

After riding in the hunt, the landlord is quite stressed, after jumping walls and knocking walls, and huffing and puffing. Then he walks towards the hen-house, and looks in the door. The maid is bent over, collecting eggs from the hens and putting them into the basket. The landlord thinks, as he begins to creep up on the girl, "Look at the rump a that, I never saw nicer. Her husband would love to kill me, he thinks I'm screwing him with the rent. I'm not a bad old chap, I put money into the community, I built schools and churches, and if the need arises, I can change from one religion to another for my own benefit. He then lifts up her dress, pulls down her bloomers, and says, "Tally-ho! Old boy!"

Co-written by Padraic and Kieran Reaney

Tell the truth and shame the devil: Ninety-nine percent of people tell lies, and one percent are lawyers. – **Padraic Reaney.**

Dream Girl

Into the night I came.
Dishevelled and wet in rain.
Humid, sweaty and no name.
Ecstasy of her black mane.

Balmy stars, the night sky lights.
Soft skin, the sensual heights.
Hungry soul, the hearts' caressed.
Curtains open dawn on Budapest.

Kieran Reaney

In relation to girls, when a man is young he gets out of bed for a rest, when he's getting old, he goes to bed for a rest. – **Padraic Reaney.**

History, But What About Her Story?

Looking down from Heaven, Irish pie, six pieces missing,
Antrim, Armagh, Derry, Down, Fermanagh, Tyrone.
Sides of a Rubik's Cube, different colours, unlucky dices,
Jigsaw picture noy becoming complete, thirty years war.

Absolute failure, doomed from the beginning,
Never going to work, like throwing a lighted match at a
Wet sod of turf, it all back-fired, agonising pain, deep hurt,
Broken people, bitterness, violence, blood-shed, hatred.

Brutal bombings, horrendous killings, don't follow
Folly, an exercise in futility, foolishness, got absolutely
No-where, Anglo-Irish agreement, Good Friday
Agreement, "Power talks, but it don't sing and dance,

And it don't walk, Forever in Blue," twenty-six
Countries? Ireland and England, rugby battle in
Croke Park, a new era, idea of a United, thirty-two
County Ireland gone and lost forever, ageing Elizabeth

Visits the island of saint and scholars – now
Unfortunately the island of hures, whores and
Robbers – first to the Republic, then to the North,
She goes home smiling, Vice-gripped hold copperfastened.

The Queen of Hearts baking tarts, and Paddy
Making hay, floodgates now open for every
Tom, Dick, or Harry? Farewell six friends, we loved
you dearly. Did anyone ever tell them that if a girl,

Is worth having, she is also worth fighting for.
History recorded – in all its different forms – never
Allows the past to die. Jesus nailed to a cross to
Save mankind – and indeed womankind – History or

His story, what about Her story?, seven super-heroes
Nailed by bullets to a cross to save Ireland,
Lonesome, heart-broken wood, His cross is every tree.
Amazing "Grace, just hold me in your arms,
And let the moment linger" …what's done is done.

Padraic Reaney

Good Answer: A wise and witty man was once asked, How long did he think a Politician should stoop? His humourous reply was, "How high is a Jack Russell?" -**Padraic Reaney.**

A video cover of the film Jude, starring Christopher Eccleston and Kate Winslet, based on the Thomas Hardy novel, depicting, at the start of the film, the rawness of rural life in the Unite Kingdom, in olden times, and indeed as it always was out the country.

Pork Chopped

It was a bitterly cold, frosty morning with a biting wind, playing around with the soft crystals of ice that were clinging on delicately to the pine trees, as they hung on for their dear life, in the back garden behind our house. It was mid-Winter, 1969, Christmas was just around the corner, and our pet pig Greeskeen could never have envisaged that his harmless life, and soul as white as the driven snow, would all be ended abruptly and quickly in dramatic fashion. In animal life, just like human life, there are lots of things, that quite frankly, there is no easy way of doing.

The killing of a pig was just one of those arduous farming jobs, that were not for the squeamish or faint-hearted. My twin brother and my-self were only six years old at the time, but it was very ironic that our grand grandmother, who was obviously decades older, could not handle it all. As a result, from early that morning "Gentle Annie" had gone to visit her brother and sister in the farm-house, a half-mile down the road and gone to bed, put her head under the pillow, to avoid hearing the sad and lonely last cries of a squealing grunter. A brutal end to a happy and innocent guzzler she always thought. Latter that evening she would return home, less upset and more relaxed, as all the glory details had been competently taken care of. She would now be looking forward to helping prepare a parcel of meat for all the neighboring families in the village, as that was the tradition in those times.

This is just one example of the cold rawness, sometimes barbarous and often startling reality of life out the country, but it was all part of the job, and there are so many other tough farming experiences you could write a book about them. This was particularly true in the West of Ireland, which was influenced greatly by the wide, wild Atlantic Ocean lashing on its coast line. But it was this hardship, in the Winter time, coupled with its aesthetic and breath-taking beauty in the Summer time that was the inspiration for many great Irish writers.

Rural life in England, Scotland, Wales and Northern Ireland would be fairly similar to that in the Republic of Ireland. This uncompromising chilly crudeness is brilliantly explored in the first part of the film Jude, which is based on Thomas Hardy's classic novel. It is directed by Michael Winterbottom and stars Christopher Eccleston, Kate Winslet, Rachel Griffiths and is highly recommended.

Padraic Reaney

Action-Reaction: the way the human mind works, in both males and females, is that it spends much more time reacting to certain events that happen to the person, rather than when the actual event itself happened. – **Padraic Reaney.**

The Bar Maid

"Where is that hammering? Lord let him in."
Like a renegade stranger, he'll get his fill.
The roasted breast of a buxom beauty fair.
The wolfhound gnaws at the bone thrown there.

Tumblers of ale, and a warm fire nice.
There's a bedroom upstairs, hope it will suffice.
Then the other lad, running home he went.
His young, tortured soul, and his hair unkempt.

The sideburns are split by waves of tears.
Of a shattered heart, and the burning fears.
When the morning comes, once again he'll dare.
Where all men go, but only few beware.

Kieran Reaney

Girls know how to lay master bait. - **Padraic Reaney.**

Change Isn't Always A Good Thing

In any and every aspect of life, very often you hear many people talking about change, change this, change that and change the other. This is amazingly not confined to bad times because some people ironically cry out for change in days of boom and zoom. Change for the sake of change can lead to a futile future and all these situations need to be thought out clearly, weighing up the pros and cons. If a person is not happy in Galway, more than likely they won't be happy in any other part of the world either. As they say, "Happiness is an inside job" and "Far away hills are green but bare", and in some extreme cases the person could be going from the frying pan to the fire. Life is like a football match, no matter how good a team is, they won't be able to attack all the time, and sometimes they might have to soak up the pressure and defend stoutly. A person might be accepting what they should change or trying to change what they should accept. In the final analysis the key to it all is "The wisdom to know the difference".

Padraic Reaney

Everything in this country has gone so horribly wrong it has deteriorated into a deplorable, diabolical, ludicrous farce. – **Padraic Reaney.**

Triumph Of The Cross. *The Round Cross at the left of the entrance to Our Lady's Holy Well.*

Young Heart Skipping A Beat

Penny, eight years old, local national school.
Head over heels in love, besotted, smitten.
She wanted him with all the madness of her soul.
Deeply and truly she would do anything for him.

Thinking about him all the time, she could not resist him.
He was cool, calm, relaxed, happy, great sense of humour.
Delightful attitude, always helping people, a beautiful mind.
Who could blame her, he had a heart of gold.

She dreamt about seducing him with sweet love hearts.
Longing for mid-week afternoons, all school work done.
Sitting excitedly, super-glued to the television.
The magic of anticipation. Then he would appear,
In all his glory … Skippy, the Bush Kangaroo.

Padraic Reaney

In the animal kingdom, the human being, man and woman, the last to be created were supposed to be the best, nicest, most good and most righteous of all, but this complex, complicated and sophisticated being is ironically the worst animal of the lot. – **Padraic Reaney.**

The Choice Is Yours

To follow God, to renounce satan.
To be inspired by acts of goodness.
To reject badness and evil.
To be a lover, not a bully or spoiler.

To learn that in giving we receive.
To realise the ultimate folly,
Of the greedy taker.
Don't get too attached to the land,
Life or anything therein.

All Jesus had was the manger in a stable.
All the human being is eventually,
Destined to have is,

The six foot by three foot.
This life is only about shadow boxing.
A trail un, to assess a person's true worth.
We're only passing through, you don't
Bring anything with you to the eternal life,

God has promised for his faithful people.
We're given free will, don't blow it.
The person that follows God,
Has no fear and will never go wrong.

Padraic Reaney

*Strong spirit: If a person hasn't got something that they believe in, to hold on to, to cling to, especially in very difficult times, they'll get destroyed very quickly. – **Padraic Reaney.***

John Wayne and Maureen O'Hara in The Quiet Man Statue unveiled in Cong, Co. Mayo on the 6th of October 2013. The Quiet Man was directed by John Ford in 1951, who was American by birth but the youngest child of Irish immigrant parents, the Feeney's from Spiddal, Co. Galway. John Ford was a great friend of Lord Killanin, who lived with his family in Spiddal House until 1960 when they sold the house. One of Lord Killanin's sons, Redmond

Morris the highly successful Hollywood film producer, was third assistant director of Alfred the Great in 1968, a substantial part of the film was shot on Knockma Hill in Caherlistrane. Photograph courtesy of Elizabeth Toher.

Deep Soul

Majestic Mayo, Green and Red, unique and special.
Pieces of joy, joy of peace, spiritual, religious.
Saint Patrick, Croagh Patrick, Croke Park.
Three Leafed Shamrock, The Blessed Trinity.

Three persons in one God, the Father,
The Son and the Holy Spirit.
April 1879, Michael Davitt, Land League
Founded, Irishtown. August 1879,

Blessed Virgin Mary, Knock Shrine, Apparition.
Early 1950s, 50-51, Senior football two-in-a-row.
1951, The Quiet Man, Cong, an iconic slice of
Old Ireland. Inisfree, an idyllic retreat island

Of saints and scholars. A haven of niceness,
Goodness and righteousness, shy innocence.
Yet untarnished by the big, bad, mad world, satan
And his sick, evil ways. Knock Airport,

Monsignor James Horan, true leader of outstanding
Resilience, flown first-class to Heaven's Gate,
Knocked on Heaven's Door. His soul now
Enjoying its reward, having reached the

Promised Land. James Horan and Mayo
Senior football team, glimpsing this
Elusive place and great dream, come on Mayo.
Get up for the cup, bring home Sam.

Padraic Reaney

The higher up "The Reek" you get, the tougher it is, but the "sweeter" the minerals. – **Kieran Reaney.**

Hail Glorious St. Patrick

St. Patrick, Principal Patron Saint of Ireland, was born in Britain or maybe Wales circa 385 AD. When he was sweet sixteen he was captured by a plundering and raiding group, and brought to Ireland, which obviously would be a very traumatic scenario for a boy of such tender years. These pirates that took him captive were led by High King, Niall of the Nine Hostages, who then sold Patrick as a slave. During all this time he showed remarkable courage, strength and resilience.

St. Patrick *(picture above) built the old Church in Donaghpatrick (Domhnach Phádraig) Cemetery in Caherlistrane in the 5th century. Domhnach is the Irish for church, St. Patrick's Church. St. Patrick's Day card (above) designed, painted and produced in art form by Kieran Reaney.*

On Slemish Mountain, in County Antrim, he worked for the following six years, under terrible, brutal conditions, as a herdsman and shepherd. In spite of his hardship, he never lost faith, and continuously and diligently prayed to God for help. One particular day he heard a voice telling him to go where a ship was waiting for him, to bring him home where he would be free. He did not hesitate, he followed what the voice had told him, escaped his nightmare hell, and returned safely home.

However, a number of years later, he had a vision to return to Ireland to begin his real mission in life, which was the conversion of pagans. For anybody and everybody, in any and every aspect of life, it is very easy to understand how difficult it would be, to return to a very painful, hell-hole of a situation, and most people would never want to hear about it again.

Patrick, saw it differently however, and with utter and total conviction, commitment and self-belief, and with God guiding and directing him, he returned to Ireland. He was then a Bishop, when he came back in a missionary capacity in 432 AD. In that aforementioned vision, he saw and heard the Irish people crying out and asking him, to come and walk once more among them. He agreed with out-stretched arms and never again left their shores.

With great enthusiasm he immediately began his Christian missionary work, and one of the first churches that he built was at Saul, in Co. Down. An Anglican church was built there in 1932, to commemorate the 1500th anniversary of the saint's arrival, and at the present time it is a pilgrimage centre visited by people of all denominations. That same year, 1932, the Eucharistic Congress was held in Ireland, and again last year in 2012, eighty years later.

Early in his missionary career, he lit a paschal fire, at Easter time on the hill of Slane, just across from the Hill of Tara, which was where the High King of Ireland had his seat. Eventually St. Patrick converted him, and during the following years he converted thousands of people to the new faith, as the floodgates of opportunity had been opened up to him, regarding his missionary work. He continued on his beautiful journey by visiting many parts of Ireland, and has an association with a huge number of monastic sites and settlements. Part of this inspirational expedition took him to different places in North Galway, and indeed Co. Galway, and of course to Croagh Patrick, or locally called the Reek, that monumental mountain in Co. Mayo, which carries the weight of mammoth religious and spiritual significance. Obviously still a place of pilgrimage, he prayed and fasted for his Irish converts on this holy mountain.

From a distance. *A panoramic view from Cave Hill in Caherlistrane, taken between Joe Flanagan's house and Oliver Curley's, with Croagh Patrick in County Mayo, barely visible on the horizon near centre of picture.*

Even though there are not many details of St. Patrick's life available, his richness in giving and strong, powerful personality and character come across vividly to us in his two writings, and in my opinion he was the first real Irish writer. The Confession, which was written in his old age, is a celebration of God's grace at work in him, which had a huge influence on him since he was young, and his writing is also a defence of his ministry. The Letter To Coroticus is an angry, indignant letter to a pirate, who had murdered some of his converts and enslave others. Who says that nice, good and righteous people never get angry? The real lover of God is a fighter, and a person that says that they never get angry means that their mind is not working right. They say that anger turned inwards causes depression, and who wants to get depressed? A third important work titled Breastplate Of St. Patrick, contrary to what some people think, was not written by St. Patrick, but several hundred years after his death. Nonetheless it faithfully reflects his true spirit, and the way in which his followers have seen and accepted his peaceful, spiritual message.

Lough Derg. *St. Patrick's Purgatory Pilgrimage Site, Purgatorium Sancti Patricii, Petiigo, Co. Donegal. This Island is visited by thousands of people each year where they fast and pray for themselves and others. They return to their homes glad that they went, grateful for the people they met and the opportunities offered to them while there. They promise to remain 'connected' with the Sanctuary by including in their prayers the intentions of all who are part of the Lough Derg story.*

St. Patrick is venerated, and on the 17th of March every year, his memory is recalled and celebrated in cities, towns and rural parishes all over Ireland, and indeed in different places all over the world, due to the phenomenal popularity of this lovable saint, as so many people are impressed by his Christian message. He will always be remembered for the vision that inspired him, in his unrelenting service of God, and by doing God's will, by converting the Irish people whom he evangelised.

It is believed that the first ever St. Patrick's Day parade actually took place in New York City, in the United States in 1762. The first St. Patrick's Day parade in the Irish Free State was held in Dublin in 1903. As part of the St. Patrick's Day celebrations, in Galway City in 1920, a brilliant film titled In The Days Of St. Patrick was shown in the Cinema. There were full houses and you could hear a pin drop.

He died circa 460 AD, possibly on the 17th of march, and his place of burial is believed to be in Downpatrick, Co. Down. The way our beloved island of Ireland has gone down so disastrously and desperately badly, especially in recent years, and is in such a terrible, very painful state, the old school of thought needs to be revisited immediately, as the Irish people are crying out for direction, leadership and inspiration, once again, almost 16 centuries later.

Padraic Reaney

Snakes and Ladders: *A snake takes a person down to satan and hell. A ladder takes a person up to God and Heaven.* **– Padraic Reaney.**

Back To Learning

The ferns and the hill.
The cairns and the mill.
The raucous and the lobster.
The locust and the posture.

The leading pathway and wood.
The fallow dear has stood.
The buzzards soar in flight.
Pine Marten's grip is tight.

Twenty-two years I did stay.
Waiting patiently for the day.
Books and pencils once again.
Where dreams they did begin.

Kieran Reaney

When people get a raw deal, they close all doors, and connections, even the slightest will be severed. **– Kieran Reaney.**

Life's A Bitch And Then He Married Wan

"Will you go easy, you'll burst a tyre, you're driving the heart out of the Ford Anglia," said Nellie to Bill as they approached town to do shopping. Bill and Nellie were both in their mid-fifties and married for twenty years. Bill was a farmer, and loved to get a break from it by going to town with Nellie. He Used to wash and shave every day and was always ready, despite working hard and long hours on the farm. He always tried to be light-hearted in a tensed situation to avoid strong emotion, but recently Nellie was becoming very irritating.

"That sweet-cake and biscuits are nice," said Bill as they were buying the groceries. But Nellie thought they were two expensive and weren't a necessity.

They ended up coming out of the shop with only tea and sugar after having a little argument. From that day on Bill wasn't washing or shaving regularly and seemed to have lost interest in a certain things like football and hurling. Nellie said, "You aren't washing or shaving every day, but you never miss 'one' and 'two'," Bill began to smile, and he said, "'One' and 'two' no more than the tea and sugar are a necessity but the rest are optional extras like in car insurance!" Nellie was awfully cold in bed, like an iceberg, she would sink the Titanic.

The following evening when they were having tea, their dog, Rupert, was jumping up on Bill trying to get something to eat. "What's wrong with you?" said Nellie, "You aren't able to put manners on that dog." Then suddenly, Rupert, in all his enthusiasm to get a piece of bread, his tail hit a cup and put it flying from the table and it broke when it hit the floor. Bill stood up, looked at Rupert and said, 'That's once."

The following morning Rupert knocked a little boy off his bicycle on his way to school, and Bill rushed out, looked at Rupert and said, "That's twice." They were all in bad form after that for a few days until one evening Bill told Nellie the sheep needed to be dosed. The two of them headed off to the field and they brought Rupert with them. When they arrived at the field Rupert made a mad dash after the sheep and he wouldn't stop or come back no matter how much Bill roared at him. He ended up driving all the sheep over a wall, into a neighbour's field and knocking a cart-gap.

Bill looked at Nellie, and said, "Stay there you." He walked down to the house and he came back with a shotgun in one hand and a spade in the other. Rupert was lying down about ten yards from Nellie and Bill shot him. Bill then rounded up the sheep and built the wall. They dosed the sheep and bill got the spade and buried Rupert. It was a very cold evening and they headed for home. They were about halfway down the road when Nellie exploded and blinded bill out of it. When she was finished, Bill looked at Nellie and he said, "That's once."

Kieran Reaney

Sooner or later, as a man is getting older, he begins to feel like the character which was brilliant played by Marlon Brando, in the classic film Last Tango In Paris, made in 1972, which was a masterpiece of cinema, directed by the great Italian expert Bernardo Bertolucci. **– Kieran Reaney.**

Broke and Broken

This world, planet earth, life on it and all its inhabitants – human beings and otherwise – was never perfect in the past, most definitely isn't perfect at the present time, nor never will be perfect in the future. Even if it was perfect, more than likely, a lot of people would find this boring. There will always be someone to rock the boat, stir up trouble, take an un-provoked lash at someone, or throw a spanner in the works. It's impossible to make some people happy. This is just the way it is.

To be perfectly honest, the celebration of the Gathering 2013, all around the country, was all about how things should be, rather than how they actually are. The way they actually are is a million miles away from the way they should be. Many Irish people are in denial, they can't face up to or handle the truth, or indeed reality.

The very bad and poor – in all aspects in the word – state of our country, was not what the parents and grand-parents of all Irish people, worked very hard for, in the past, often losing blood, seat and tears and the Irish people of the present time certainly deserve much better than this. This most definitely was not what the seven super-heroes died for in 1916. God Save Ireland. God Bless You All.

Padraic Reaney

What some people see as negativity and cynicism, other people see as realism and honesty. – **Padraic Reaney.**

Soulful Scenarios

From the ashes of pain, hurt, heartache, unfairness and injustice a very great and beautiful thing can be born. In Ireland in the 1800s, in the post famine years – for almost thirty years in fact -the people and their country were totally and utterly destroyed and annihilated. This human misery and suffering change dramatically in August, 1879, with the Apparition in the small village of knock, in Co. mayo, of the Blessed Virgin Mary. Just over five years and two months later, on the 1st of November, 1884, the G.A.A.- the greatest form of Community Development ever in this country – was founded. Yes, you said it, the 1st of November, is of course, All Saints Day.

Last year, in 2012 the Connacht G.A.A. Centre of Excellence was opened not too far away from this world-wide famous village of Knock. Also this magnificent miracle in Knock, of Heavenly spirituality, was part of the inspiration of the great revival of Irish writing. As part of the Centenary celebrations of Knock Shrine, in late September and early October 1979, Pope John Paul II visited Ireland, which was a never to be forgotten, astonishingly soulful and up-lifting experience.

Padraic Reaney

As regards anything and everything in the universe, this world planet earth, and all life and otherwise in it, on it and outside it, including the human race and all its associated complexities, it is all connected because it all came from the one, same source, God. – **Padraic Reaney.**

Throw't In Ref!

It is my total and utter belief that this great event, the visit of Pope John Paul II to Ireland in 1979, part of which took place in the famous Ballybrit Racecourse, on the outskirts of Galway city, inspired the giants of Galway hurling Castlegar to soldier forward, and win the All-Ireland senior club championship title, giving reknowned "Cashel" the unique distinction of being the first club from the County Galway to achieve this wonderful dream.

Also it is my firm belief that the fulfilling of this ambition led to Galway senior hurlers winning the All-Ireland Championship that same year in 1980, after a 57 year very long wait, and this is due course led to the 1980s being the best decade ever for Galway hurling. It could accurately be stated that this was a Cuchuliann era for the helmet-clad warriors using sticks and sliotars, in the Maroon and White county in the West. Corner-stones of both teams, the legendary Connolly brothers are folk-heroes ever since, and undoubtedly one of the most remarkably talented and skillful, aristocratic sporting families ever to come to Co. Galway.

In the coming months, over thirty-four years later Pope John Paul II is to be canonized a saint. People of Ireland we love you, as well all look forward to be a bright, brand new day ... and sincerely hope that the next boom and zoom period in Irish history is built on solid rock, and not quick sand.

Padraic Reaney

In any and every aspect of life, when a person or people achieve success, this achievement is done, first and foremost for the person or people themselves, and obviously for their family and friends, their parish, county, province and country but most of all and ultimately they do it for God. – **Padraic Reaney.**

Come On! Caman!

In the G.A.A. there are days a person really enjoys and remembers, and other days may not be as good. But there is one day I still remember quite well, when my twin brother Padraic, our father Tommy and myself went to see the All-Ireland Senior Club Hurling Championship semi-final between Castlegar (Galway) and Blackrock (Cork) which was played in Athenry, in mid-April 1980.

The Cork inter-county senior hurling team had won the National League final the previous Sunday, and Blackrock had seven of that team, and also Kilkenny midfielder, Frank Cummins, playing against Castlegar. The Connolly brothers were the backbone of Castlegar, Padraic at fullback, Joe at centre half-forward, Gerry at left corner-forward, and two masterstrokes, John at centre halfback and Michael at full-forward.

There was a massive crowd, the vast majority supporting 'Cashel", and after a determined display, and a lot of good hurling, Castlegar held on for a narrow and famous victory. That day we were beside, and indeed had the pleasure of talking to a former Galway hurler, the great Mickey Burke. Castlegar went on to win the All-Ireland Club final that year against Ballycastle from Antrim.

The same day as the Castlegar/Blackrock game, another Galway Club, St. Grellan's from Ballinasloe took on St. Finbarr's from Cork in the All-Ireland Senior club Football Championship final in Tipperary Town. Unfortunately the Jimmy Barry-Murphy powered St. Finbarr's were too strong for Ballinasloe. St. Grellan's won the 1979 county Galway Senior Football Championship final against Dunmore MacHales, after a replay, and made it two-in-a-row against Corofin in 1980. The St. Grellan's team from that era was one of the classiest teams ever in the country, and in 1981 were favourites for the three-in-a-row against Milltwon.

The final was played very late in the year, in very wet and windy conditions in Tuam Stadium. Milltown got into the game from the word go, showing spirit, determination and passion and won out in the end. Jim Carney and the Milltown management team were the architects behind this victory. This year the Ballinasloe Junior football team won the All-Ireland Junior Football Championship final. Congratulations to them and to all winning teams that have 'Gathered" for success in 2013.

Kieran Reaney

Whatever is inside a person's head is also in their hands with skills and talents as regards creativity. It is only a person that really loves life to the heart that has that special power to be creative. **– Padraic Reaney.**

We'll Win It

We'll win it for David Hemmings.
The All-Ireland we should have won.
The final whistle broke our hearts.
The golden hair of Prunella Ransome.

We'll win it for Knockma Hill.
Alfred the Great, Gettyburg, Croke Park.
The crunch tackles of battle.
Reverberate now until after dark.

We'll win it for Emily Lawless.
Masterclass writer from the past.
Corn-coloured harvest hair once again.
Blue and White ribbons to the mast.

We'll win it for Lough Hackett.
The turbulent waves are placid now.
At the foot of torrid Glenshawk.
Profuse perspiration drips from the brow.

We'll win it for the men of 1890.
Castlehackett House, Hackett's Castle
And Téach Amen.
Their spirit still pervades this land.
The clashing sword and the pen.

We'll win it for Kilcoona.
Corner Chapel, Our Lady's Holy Well.
Donaghpatrick, the centre of the parish.
St. Patrick, Caherlistrane Church and the Bell.

We'll win it for Eva O'Flaherty.
Lisdonagh House and Luimnagh Pier.
In the American Civil War.
Colonel Patrick Kelly dispelled the fear.

We'll win it for our parents and grand-parents.
When we were lost they showed us the way.
The man who loves his football.
Is always waiting for the day.

We'll win it for the Kirwan's.
The graveyards, Donaghpatrick,
Kilcoona and Abbeytown.
For the people that came before us.
Permanent tears are rolling down.

We'll win it for God Our Creator.
Outstretched hands reach for the sky.
The burning bonfires in our souls.
Beyond the stars, an Almighty high.

Kieran Reaney

Rugby Rules: *In the game of Rugby, just like in the game of life, the more committed the player is to the tackle, the less pain they feel.* – **Padraic Reaney.**

Sacred Heart Of Jesus   *Sacred Heart Of Mary*

Regress: *Sometimes going backwards is going forwards. The gifted thinking genius of the outstanding field athlete Dick Fosbury proved this, when he revolutionized the High Jump, by discovering the "Fosbury Flop" technique, which he used in the 1968 Olympic Games in Mexico City, and won the gold medal with a jump of 7ft. 4.25ins. This scintillating technique was used to great effect by multitudes world-wide ever since, in this highly entertaining event, and immediately more new heights were scaled, and in due course to such an event that was really impossible using other techniques.* – **Padraic Reaney.**

Photo©John Hinde Ltd.

Other great Irish writers' included Jonathan swift and Thomas Moore.

There are two extreme types of Psychology, namely soft Psychology and Hard Psychology. Why Hard Psychology always works is because it is very serious and people get afraid of it. A quick example of both: As regards Soft Psychology, read the story of *The Three Bears*. As regards Hard Psychology, watch the film *Full Metal Jacket (1987)*, which was directed by Stanley Kubrick who was also known as "The Master". Some of his other films include: *Spartacus* (1960), *Lolita* (1962), *Dr. Strangelove* (1964), *2001: A Space Odyssey* (1968), *A Clockwork Orange* (1971), *Barry Lyndon* (1975), *The Shining* (1980) and *Eyes Wide Shut* (1999). – **Padraic Reaney.**

Tourism in this small island country of Ireland needs to be understood far better, first and foremost, and then marked in a much greater way, because it is operating miles below its full potential. The Arts, in all its many different forms, is a fantastic means of making people more aware of all this inspirational beauty, and getting them more interested in its real depth and true meaning. Galway, city of the tribes, and Capital of the West, is now widely recognized as one of the best and most innovative cities for the art House Cinema being opened there, in early Summer next year, 2014.

A few weeks before that Kieran and Padraic Reaney's first Play which is titled After Hours Take-Off will be available, and they wish to sincerely thank Darius Ivan from the Craic in Galway magazine, and its Editor Avril Horan, for a photograph for the front cover of this Play. After all, History, Heritage, Culture, and Sport, all controlled by Spirituality of course, are all part of who we are and what we are, and should be explored a lot more, so that we can learn from the past, embrace the present and look forward to a more fulfilling future for everyone, all across the board. – **Kieran and Padraic Reaney.**

A view of Lough Corrib, near Ashford Castle, in Cong, County Mayo.

The West Of Ireland has been associated with the inspiration for many great writers down through the years and decades. In our opinion, the best ever female Irish writer was Emily Lawless (1845-1913), from Castlehackett House in Caherlistrane. She wrote 19 books, and her parents were Edward lawless and Elizabeth Kirwan. The first President of Ireland, Douglas Hyde, wrote frequently about the Kirwan's of Castlehackett and visited Caherlistrane in the early 1900s. Emily Lawless was a great friend of William Butler Yeats and Lady Augusta Gregory, who both used to write about Knockma and the Kirwan's, and Emily used to visit them in Coole Park in Gort. Oscar Wilde's father, Sir William Wilde, once said that the scenic beauty of Cong in County Mayo and Lough Corrib stretched all the way over to Knockma Hill. J.M. Synge, who was familiar with the Aran Islands, knew Emily Lawless and read her work. James Joyce was married to Galway city woman Nora Barnacle and visited Galway in 1912 and Patrick Kavanagh's girlfriend one time was Deidre Courtney from Barnaderg

The first article in this book is paying tribute to Emily Lawless

www.ingramcontent.com/pod-product-compliance
Lightning Source LLC
Chambersburg PA
CBHW071857070526
44583CB00016B/1729